Revival Worshipers For The Last Days

An Urgent Call to Deeply Know God's Glorious Nature

REVISED EDITION

Yolandita Colón

Contents

REVIVAL WORSHIPERS FOR THE LAST DAYS

First English edition published in 2020.

Minor revision in 2021, Major revision in 2024

ISBN: 978-1-964673-04-2 (Revised Edition)

This book has been updated and revised for clarity and to correct typographical errors. The original version was published in 2020, and this revised version is published in 2024.

Contact the author at: www.YolanditaColon.com

Cover design based on the original concept by Yvonne Parks (2020).
Revised edition by Yolandita Colón (2024).
Interior Design by Yolandita Colón.
Lion Ablaze image on the front cover by William Rulli,
used and modified with permission.

Printed in the United States of America
10 9 8 7 6 5 4 3 2 1

Dedication

First, I lovingly dedicate this book to the Almighty I Am Who I Am, the Origin of my life and my eternal King. This book is all about You and a tribute to You! Second, Secondly, I extend my heartfelt dedication to my loving husband, Herman, a man whose heart is aligned with God's heart. Thank you for your unwavering love and support, especially during challenging moments. Finally, to my godly sons Isaac and Lemuel. I am joyful and proud to be called your mom. I thank God for blessing me with both of you.

PART I

Chapter 1

A Deeper Revelation of Worship

When God wants to give you something enormous, it often comes in seed form. This seed grows, develops, matures through our continuous seeking, receiving, and giving in a spirit of worship.

That's how this book was born in my heart. I began my journey as an adolescent, but it was not until 2009 that I began writing it. It has taken me eleven years since then. However, the fact that the Old Testament, which consists of 39 books took almost 1,000 years, we can imagine that each book could have taken approximately 39 years to write. This realization made it clear to me that the finest writings take time to develop under God's progressive revelation, the fire of formation, and experience. Therefore, here is a book that took me eleven years to give birth to for such a time as this.

In this book, you will find valuable information about how an intimate worshiper is formed under the fire and threshing floor of the Mighty One. If you can learn this well, you can become an intimate friend of God, which will catapult you into being a revivalist to the world in the last days.

Revival can mean many things to many people. Depending on your understanding or experience, you might think of revival as either negative or positive. When I say revival, I mean a spiritual reawakening of love for the Bridegroom and an heightened awareness of who He truly is and your significance to Him. Revival is a place of holy intimacy with our Most Holy God that becomes your main focus and priority in life. It is a new and divine romance with our Creator. In simpler words, revival is a renewed awareness and reverence for His holiness that suddenly causes everything else to become secondary and less important. One of the essences of revival Is to lead us to do mighty things for the Lord.

THE ROOTS OF MY REVIVAL

Since I was very young, I have had an unshakable passion to wholeheartedly serve the Lord. I loved singing and was eager to learn and share the word of God. I felt a strong calling for ministry. I dreamed of attending college to study music and the Bible, a dream I held onto every day despite the odds not being in my favor.

Living as a naïve girl in a secluded island town, isolated from the wider world, I was unsure if such things even existed. Yet, I was always a big dreamer, holding onto the belief that with God, nothing was impossible.

I was raised in Puerto Rico from the age of seven until I was sixteen years old—my formative years. We lived in a small town in the country in Guayanilla, Puerto Rico. I attended a campus church in my community that was part of a growing ministry in our small downtown city, or what we called "El Pueblo."

From the age of eleven, I eagerly walked a mile to join the 6:00 am prayers with the elders at our small country church. Each morning, I woke up early to attend these prayer sessions before heading to school, undeterred by the fact that I was always the youngest there. My hunger for God transcended any concerns about age differences. I didn't care about age; if anything, I wanted to learn more from older people, as those around my age didn't have a clue and weren't as hungry as I was. The older folks always told me that God had something big in store for my life because they had never seen a young person as hungry as I was. All I wanted was to encounter God.

Despite my youth, I sensed there had to be something more. I yearned for God to reveal Himself to me and to use me for His divine purposes. Frequently, I spent three to four hours praying in my bedroom, where I had awesome encounters with God. My heart prayer was, 'Lord, use me for Your purposes.' The call of God was burning in my heart so fervently that it would often keep me awake through the early morning hours. I would spend that time reading the Bible and speaking in tongues. I also continually pray, "Lord, please help me sing better so I can one day play piano and worship you skillfully. During that time, my parent's financial situation was incredibly scarce, and my parents couldn't afford to purchase a piano for me or arrange for voice lessons. Nonetheless, my passion remained unquenchable.

In Puerto Rico, there existed a children's radio ministry known as "Joyas de Cristo" (Jewels of Christ). Through this radio program, remarkably talented children as young as three years old would sing, preach, and traveled across the island as part of this ministry. The impact of 'Joyas de Cristo' left such a profound mark on me that I often dreamt of being used by God like those children.

The Holy Spirit has been preparing me for this lifelong journey—a path I continue to tread—because I've come to understand that God always has more to reveal to me. His continuous revelation knows no bounds and is truly limitless.

From the age of eight, I had a deep love for singing to the Lord. I eagerly seized every opportunity to sing at nearly every service. However, when I was twelve years old, an older sister in Christ took it upon herself to criticize and question my intentions. She subjected me to hurtful remarks, and I couldn't help but feel that it was a malicious attempt to silence me. Tears welled up in my eyes, and I seriously contemplated giving up. Fortunately, one of the main leaders noticed my distress, offered words of encouragement, and prayed for me. In that moment, I felt the comforting presence of the Lord, and from that day on I resolved not to allow anything or anyone to hinder me from singing to Him.

At home, I sang all the time, climbing on top of the swing slide in my house's backyard and singing fearlessly like a rooster. However, despite my love for singing to God and my hunger for His word, I realized that I still needed a deeper understanding of the kind of worship that could usher in true revival.

NO REVELATION ABOUT TRUE WORSHIP

The small church I used to attend was on the side of legalism—meaning that there was a lot of fear of man, man-made rules, and because of this the Spirit of God was stifled. What little we knew about music had more to do with performance than worship. There were only a few transient musicians who played, along with a few amateur and untrained musicians, but there was a lack of revelation about the true meaning of worship. We were on minus zero.

At age twelve, I became the main singer of a Christian band. That was when I started singing at Christian events and gatherings. It felt exciting to have the opportunity to sing in different places, but sadly, we were singing and playing without revelation. It was just special music—nothing out of the ordinary, nothing profound, only entertainment. We spent hours and hours just rehearsing cuts, styles, and songs but never spent significant time in prayer or the word as a team. Of course, I had no idea how significant true worship was because no one had ever taught me about intimate prophetic worship. I had not even heard of such kind of worship.

I began to notice a significant shortage of trained musicians in the Spanish churches within the music ministry. At times, the pastors' desperation led them to select individuals who could barely play two chords. They would even assign people to lead in singing, even though these individuals could not hold a tone, much less understand the essence of the worship ministry. Even many pastors seemed to lack the revelation of how vital the ministry of worship is within the church.

Over the years, I've heard statements like, 'Music is not a ministry!' or 'Preaching is more important, even without worship!

Others commented, "Slow worship puts us to sleep; we prefer fast-paced songs!"

At times, a rapid succession of short, upbeat praise songs known as "Cadena de coritos" would be sung incessantly for an hour or even longer, often continuing until the "Spirit fell."

This practice was also referred to as "los coritos de avivamiento" or "coritos del ayer" (the revival praise songs or the songs of yesteryears).

I remember seeing leaders yawning and falling asleep during worship time. Sometimes, when musicians were in a church, I would see more of a competition of talents, egos, pride, and carnality more than anything else.

There was no revelation about true worship. I don't blame them since there was never any spiritual training for worshipers, not even a class about worship. We were never trained in the importance of becoming genuine worshipers of the Father, perhaps because there was a lack of understanding regarding what Jesus conveyed in John 4:23–24 on this very topic: the worship of true revival.

A DREAM IS CONCEIVED

As a result, a desire formed in my heart: "One day, once I finish studying music, I will start a music school for all the churches that need musicians and singers." With this strategy, I will be able to raise musicians for churches in need!" But little did I know that I still had a long way to go before solidifying the dream God had put in my heart. I still needed much more of the revelation of God's word and His design for worship in the last days. I had no idea how this was going to unfold and how it was going to look in the end. I only knew it was a burden in my heart, and I felt called to solve this deficiency.

Sometimes we have a burden or passion in our hearts, but we have no idea how it will look in the end because our thoughts and ways are so limited. The scripture states this clearly, "'My thoughts are nothing like your thoughts,' says the Lord. 'And my ways are far beyond anything you could imagine. For just as the heavens are higher than the earth, so my ways are higher than your ways and my thoughts higher than your thoughts' " (Isaiah 55:8–9).

When I was sixteen, my dad lost his primary source of income, and my parents decided to move to Long Branch, New Jersey. While I was there, I started going to a little Hispanic church. I immediately began serving wherever there was a need, as I always loved serving God. Within this community of believers, the focus primarily centered around teaching the Word and evangelism. However, there seemed to be a gap in their understanding regarding the power of worship and its crucial role in directing our hearts toward the Lord.

When I turned sixteen, my dad lost his main source of income, prompting my parents to make the decision to relocate to Long Branch, New Jersey. During my time there, I began attending a small Hispanic church. My passion for serving God led me to immediately offer my assistance wherever there was a need.

There was a deficiency of musicians there, just as in my home church in Puerto Rico, except for one young man who played a twelve-string guitar. Despite his skill, there still was no profound revelation about who God was. There was no focus on worship. It saddened my heart.

One day, I told a small group of congregants about my vision for the worship ministry and how I hoped to study music and start a music school to train music ministers. I recall how they taunted, laughed, and stared at me as if I were insane or from another world. In my naive and fragile sixteen-year-old heart, I felt like my world was torn apart. It trembled my faith. But inside of me, I had a strong determination to fulfill my dream—God's dream for His church, to raise true worshippers for the Father.

At age seventeen, I moved to Long Island, New York, where I met some excellent musicians. I became a part of a Christian band, and we made an album together. When I was twenty, I made my first album with all original songs. It was called *Hija del Rey* (*The King's Daughter*).

Certain carnal Christians criticized my chosen title because they deemed it presumptuous for me to claim the status of a king's daughter. All these experiences should provide you with insight into the scope of influence I had to contend with throughout my life. Nevertheless, I remained resolute in my conviction. I understood, even if only to a limited extent at that time, that I possessed a heritage of royalty through Jesus Christ. I was, indeed, a daughter of the King of kings and the Lord of lords. This understanding unfolded progressively, however, I often felt misplaced in contexts that did not contribute to my growth. However, God was aware of my journey and had a flawless plan in place.

During this period, despite numerous obstacles such as language barriers, financial constraints, and hardships, I finally obtained my G.E.D. My life circumstances had previously hindered me from completing a traditional high school education.

Moving on to college brought me closer to my dream of studying music, but it was not without its challenges. Initially, my focus was on studying music, but it excluded the study of God's Word (the Bible) because the college I attended was secular. Additionally, I juggled evening work with daytime classes. There were moments when I dozed off while driving to and from college, risking car accidents, but God protected me. My college journey spanned locations in New York and Puerto Rico as I strived to secure enough funds to sustain myself. My parents withheld their support due to their disagreement with my choice to pursue a music education. This isn't meant as criticism toward them; they simply had reservations about my path. If I had chosen a different profession, they might have supported me. I was the first in my family to attend a university, and their intentions were rooted in their vision of what constituted a good life.

Nonetheless, I explored every possible avenue, including selling my car to fund my last semester I could afford. However, the accumulated difficulties eventually forced me to drop out due to a lack of financial resources. I felt so grieved. I cried, wept, prayed, and waiting for a breakthrough for three years.

. . .

ON GOD'S PATH AGAIN

I met my loving husband three years after this. We got married, and a year later, we moved to Springfield, Missouri. It was there I was able to resume my studies again. My loving husband, Herman, wholeheartedly supported my educational journey throughout college in numerous ways, something I will always remember and forever appreciate.

I initially enrolled in a Christian college, but after a year, I shifted my focus to people and grew disheartened by the prevailing religious spirit within the institution. So, I decided to go to a secular university instead. I was there for three years, learning much about music and pushing through barriers like my limited understanding of English colloquialisms and culture shock.

During that time, I was able, by the grace of God, to make yet another music album with all original songs. However, I was still short of revelation about true holy worship, and though I feel that I sang with all my heart, I did it without a deep revelation about intimate and holy worship—the one the Father seeks in us.

I was feeling dissatisfied in my soul, so I started a forty-day fast with my husband to seek the will of God and get guidance from Him. One day, while I was in my music history class, the Holy Spirit, in His very sweet, quiet voice, whispered into my Spirit, "You know that I did not call you to be in this school. I called you for the ministry."

I immediately said, *What?* Suddenly, the Holy Spirit opened my eyes so I could see what I had done—three years out of His will!

I felt broken. I ran to the restroom, closed myself in a stall, and there I cried in repentance for the remainder of my class. I could not stop crying and asking God to forgive me for my disobedience and for putting my eyes on men rather than on

Him. I promised Him I would obey Him and leave that school to attend a Christian college where I could learn about worship ministry. Mind you, I was already in my senior year and part of the Honor Society. But when I made that sacrificial decision, the Lord started opening doors.

More than that, little did I know the huge surprise that was ahead. Shortly after my decision, I discovered I was four months pregnant with my first baby. Then, God called us to start a church in Faribault, Minnesota, with a group of eight people. It was a radical move that changed the course of my life.

My husband was on the board of regents of North Central University. We knew then that any board of regents' dependent could attend this school under a full scholarship, but this only included children; it did not include their spouses. God worked the biggest miracle I have ever seen; I was accepted into North Central University with a scholarship to pay for all tuition, with enough left to cover my books. This was the main sign we had put before the Lord. The university had never done this. It was the first time in 75 years they made such an exception. They allowed me—the wife—to attend school fully paid as a dependent of a board member instead of limiting it to only a son or daughter. I also found out after many years that I was the *only one* ever to get that kind of scholarship. God moved mountains for me because He had a perfect plan, and His plan was powerfully unfolding little by little in my life. He was waiting for me to decide to change my mind and obey at any cost. The cost included many huge life changes, but it was all worth it! He was bringing me through a funneling effect into His perfect plan.

We moved, I started attending NCU, and I was six months pregnant. I traveled almost every day to Minneapolis from Faribault for two years (about an hour drive without traffic). It was a challenge, especially with my pregnancy, snowstorms, distance, home, and the ministry waiting for me after I got back to Faribault every time. But I was determined that even if this was the last thing I did in my life, I would accomplish my dream and finish my studies. I felt the strong call and was determined to study music/worship and the Bible. I was going to accomplish my long-time dream, held since I was eight years old, to start a music school for ministers. This dream was finally born in the summer of 2000, and I called it 'La Escuela de Música Ministerial' (LEMM) ('The School of Music Ministers') at our small church in Faribault.

THE DAY MY WORSHIP BECAME SUPERNATURAL

Back at the university, I had a professor who was one of my best music instructors. Through his teachings, I learned so much about worship for the first time in my life. I was like a sponge in every one of his classes. I was so inspired and enthralled by his teachings and his heart of worship. I loved how he poured out his heart in worship while skillfully playing his piano. I had never encountered this kind of worshiper. This inspired me to a profoundly transformative journey, one that took me into realms previously unimagined.

One day as I was leading worship in our regular church service in Faribault, something unusual happened. As I was worshiping with all my heart, the heavens opened, and I started prophesying through my singing.

I felt awkward for a minute. I thought to myself, *Am I going crazy? What is this?* I had never heard or seen anyone do this, not even my worship professor, as anointed as he was when he worshiped. Even my husband was wondering what this was about. I was puzzled. The power of God was tangible, and the prophetic words kept coming through my singing and worshiping. It was something new and scary because I was afraid that I was becoming unbiblical in my worship.

I searched the scriptures to see if I could find more information about this. I even Googled the words "prophetic worship" to see if this was happening in other places. Google only had a few things that came back as prophetic worship, but it was more of an African American style of worship, not the kind of prophetic worship I had encountered and experienced. I thought to myself, *could this be a new move of God?* I was puzzled but very intrigued as to where God was taking me with this. I still needed more revelation about this revival worship.

In one of my classes at NCU, we studied all the revivals of the world. During this class, I gained an understanding of the essential similarities in all these revivals. One similarity was a new anointed sound in worship and prayer that God released in every one of those revivals. The second was even more shocking: each of those revivals was stifled or crippled by Christian murmurers, or should I say, gossip worshipers.

I realized how significant and vital our words are in the spiritual realm. Words have the power to either destroy or revive what God is doing. (see Ezekiel 37:4-6) True worshipers, therefore, are critical to maintaining and nurturing revivals. However, gossiping or murmuring was also a kind of devotion. More specifically, it was (usually unintentional) demon worship. I realized that a person was either a worshiper or a gossiper and that many well-intentioned murmuring Christians had crippled, murdered, or assassinated revivals in history, dating back to the time of Moses in the desert. The Bible tells us not to grieve the Holy Spirit of God, which is exactly what occurred in numerous revivals when people started to grumble. This was the beginning of the journey that led me to write my first book, *El Asesino del Avivamiento* (*The Killer of Revival*).

I started the music school LEMM in 2001 with forty-five

students. I was able to use this school as my senior project, and I graduated in May of 2001. I was so excited! I was growing along with my students. This experience started a revolution in my heart and the hearts of my students.

I continued this school until 2003, when I almost died while giving birth to my second son, Lemuel. They did two major surgeries on me that left me weak, and it took me approximately two years to recuperate physically and especially emotionally. Thankfully, my son was resurrected, and my life was supernaturally protected. God was greatly merciful and good to us. And even through this hard time, God had a plan. He allowed this circumstance to draw me more into His presence, redeeming the suffering of that season. Honestly, though, I thought it was the end because that is how it felt.

NEW CHALLENGES, NEW GROWTH

Another transition occurred after nine years in Faribault when God called us to move to Minneapolis and pastor Maranatha Minneapolis church. In June 2008, we began our pastoral journey in Minneapolis, Minnesota. Upon arriving, I received a clear message from God that the key to our success in this new environment was to deepen my commitment to prayer and fasting while maintaining my focus on Him. Although life in the city and the ministry presented various challenges, our determination to follow God's guidance remained unwavering.

The church faced difficulties stemming from past issues with previous leadership before our arrival, making our initial days in ministry challenging. We encountered dysfunction and opposition from some of the leaders there. However, we continued to trust in the Lord's plan and persevered, recognizing that this was yet another phase of growth orchestrated by God. We had to grow through yet another funneling process of God.

During that time of trial, my husband and I started getting involved in a ministry called RAIN Ministries with their monthly healing institutes. In my heart, I had the desire to serve another woman of God. I have always felt that it is important for every worshiper to keep their heart humble—looking to other men and women of God for inspiration and impartation, just like Onesiphorus was refreshed in his walk with God by the Apostle Paul. That's how this ministry became for my husband and me as we served the Apostles Richards for a time.

Through these monthly healing institutes, as I ministered in worship, the Lord would speak to and minister to our hearts each time. This was a way in which God manifested Himself to us, giving us encouragement, direction, vision, and comfort through those difficult and painful times.

I also saw beautiful signs of growth when the Lord began to give me a new anointed and fresh song every month. These songs were unleashed during my time with God in the Holy Spirit's room, where I prayed and groaned, often until the early hours of the morning.

The *Holy Spirit room* is a room that I dedicated to the Lord since 2004. This dedicated room was a place of encounters with God, a place of weeping, and a place where I would pour my heart into Him, spend time in His word, write my books and where songs are birthed.

You can create a sacred space wherever you are. Just like the Israelites, you can meet with God by setting up your own 'tent'—a special place to encounter God in prayer and worship. This will be your personal sacred space, similar to how Moses met with God in the Tent of Meeting.

Chapter 2

The Threshing Floor of God

This work is the result of years on the threshing floor as a worshiper at the feet of Jesus. I am eternally grateful for the inspiration, wisdom, and revelation God's threshing floor has formed and produced in my life. I am thankful that through the threshing floor process, God has taught me the importance of being a true intimate worshiper of the Father. The Father is seeking those kinds of intimate worshipers for the last days.

The threshing floors were used in Bible times as a place for threshing and winnowing the sheaves of crops; it was a place for processing grains. The winnowing process involved flinging or throwing the grain up after it had been beaten off the stalks so the wind would carry away the chaff, and the wheat grain would be set free and fall to the ground. This reminds me of what John 12:24 (ESV) says, *"Unless a grain of wheat falls into the earth and dies, it remains alone, but if it dies, it bears much fruit."*

Verse 25 explains this a bit deeper. This threshing floor of God is where we can decide if we will give up our lives in this world to follow Him. If we follow him, it will produce eternal life and blessing. God's threshing floor is a place of metamorphosis and transformation.

When you are on the threshing floor, you feel like your life is at a dead end. You feel tossed up and down and broken. You are many times disappointed and brokenhearted. You feel like a train just went over you, barely alive and in pieces. As hard as it may feel, every worshiper must go through the threshing floor to become a mature and experienced worshiper who can be useful in the Kingdom of God.

A threshing floor is where God brings us through a process of purification, cleansing, and separation until we mature enough for His divine purposes. A threshing floor is a place of brokenness where He winnows the chaff out of our lives. It is an excruciating process, but its results are spiritual preparedness and maturity. Although the threshing floor is a painful place to be, it could lead you to the highest level of intimacy you would ever find. Suppose you choose to go through this process, you will come to a place of intensified intimacy with God where your worship becomes more than music, where it becomes a continual fresh encounter with who God is and a lifestyle of intimacy with His Person and Presence.

God's threshing floor is where you get a new revelation of who He is. You will never be able to return to your old self after this process. In the end, great things come from this threshing floor experience. Just as Romans 8:28 says, "We know that God causes everything to work together for the good of those who love God and are called according to His purpose for them." So, stay on the threshing floor; only good will come out of this process.

Chapter 3

A Heavenly Experience

One day, during one of our services, we were surprised by the manifestation of God that was beyond what we had ever expected or experienced. I found myself with Jesus in heaven, where He talked to me about the worship of the last days.

It was Saturday, November 14, 2009, around 7:00 pm. We were all gathering for our usual School of Discipleship evening class. When we were ready to begin, my husband started with a prayer. We planned to teach about the Holy Spirit that night, but when we started praying, something strange started happening. Herman could not begin the class despite several tries.

I was beginning to worry because we had a class to teach, or so I thought. I then went near my husband at the altar to assist him in putting on some music on my computer when all of a sudden, I felt this powerful electricity coming over me and intensifying by the minute. It was as if I had just entered an electromagnetic field. Somehow, I could see and feel in the Spirit the presence of a nine-foot angel behind us at the altar.

Zechariah's experience gives a good description of what I saw, "And an angel of the Lord appeared to him, standing to the right of the altar of incense" (Luke 1:11 NASB).

Then the Lord gave me some prophetic words for the people. Some of them were sitting down and wondering when the class would start. I told them the words that I heard the Holy Spirit say. The words were:

You have asked me for revival, *but* revival will come in a less-expected way, place, and date. Revival will come *only* to the *hungry*. The question is, if revival depended on your hunger for Me, would there be revival tonight?

I continued to pray under the heavy and glorious presence of God. The presence of God was very electrifying and powerful! We've felt the presence of God before, but this was a more profound and supernatural encounter way beyond what we had experienced before that day. We were completely immersed in His presence. I started intimately worshiping Him as I bowed down before Him in love.

A POWERFUL VISION

Suddenly, it was as if I had just died and gone to heaven by revelation. I was completely absent from the classroom at that moment. When I realized what was happening, I noticed two angels were pulling out a chair so that I would sit in front of a white, round table.

When I looked across the table, there sat Jesus, looking at me as if we were about to start a casual conversation. When I looked and realized I was in heaven and sitting in front of Him, I exclaimed, excited and in awe, "Jesus! Are you right in front of me? Jesus? It's really You! You love me? Oh, Jesus, I love You!"

And all of a sudden, the table was gone. I found myself

embracing Jesus while sitting on His lap. I was so amazed that I started kissing His hand and feet repeatedly, telling Him, "I adore You, Lord Jesus. Have you come to speak with me?"

I was amazed I was there! Jesus seemed like an average person, happy and loving. I would look at Jesus and stay in awe that He was with me. I felt unworthy of this privilege.

Nonetheless, Jesus would only look at me with eyes filled with love, and He would laugh with me, very relaxed as an intimate friend. At that moment, a divine romance song began to play on a heavenly piano, and we started dancing together in a divine and heavenly romantic dance. My face was right next to His. It was a very intimate dance. I couldn't believe Jesus would dance with me! I would hug Him, astonished that I was still alive.

There was *such* peace there that it is hard to explain. I thought about my husband and kids since I did not know if I was dead or alive as we were dancing this beautiful and awesome dance. Suddenly, Jesus transmitted this profound peace that made me feel they were under His care and that I had nothing to worry about. Something like this is described in the scriptures, "...You will experience God's peace, which exceeds anything we can understand. His peace will guard your hearts and minds as you live in Christ Jesus" (Philippians 4:7).

WHAT JESUS WANTED TO SHOW ME

In my revelation, Jesus suddenly took my hand and told me, "Come, I am going to take you to some places."

We started walking, and He took me to a crystal-clear river that flowed out of The Throne. I got excited like a little girl and found myself inside the river with Jesus. I started splashing my face with both hands with this awesome crystal-clear water. As

I splashed, I would excitedly say to Jesus, "Wow! This is precious and beautiful! Wow! Jesus! This water is so precious!"

Jesus was inside the river with me; he looked at me and laughed with me as a friend having fun with and enjoying the moment together.

The following scripture talks about the river of life that flows from the throne of God and of the Lamb through the middle of the city. This concurs with my revelation.

Then the angel showed me the river of the water of life, bright as crystal, flowing from the throne of God and of the Lamb through the middle of the street of the city; also, on either side of the river, the tree of life with its twelve kinds of fruit, yielding its fruit each month... (Revelation 22:1–3 ESV)

After this experience, He took my hand suddenly again as a close friend and told me, "Come, I am going to show you something."

He let me peek through a small door into what appeared to be a room full of heavenly flowers, but I could only see a tiny portion of it. All I remember is that they were flowers I'd never seen before, and they were difficult to describe or remember.

After this, He took my hand again and told me, "Come, I am going to reveal something to you."

We entered somewhere resembling a storehouse with drawers, similar to a records court. The square drawers were quite long. They had what appeared to be silver and gold mixed in a very fancy and elegant font written on them. He selected one of the drawers, which happened to contain my initials. Mine was just one of *many* that were present. All the drawers had initials, but He would not let me see the initials on the other drawers.

When Jesus opened the drawer with my initials, there were hundreds and hundreds of little scrolls inside it. The scrolls had golden letters written on them. Although I couldn't see the initials on the other drawers, at that moment, He gave me eyes to see inside some of the surrounding drawers. Some had three scrolls, some had one scroll, and some had just a little more than that. But when Jesus opened the drawer with my initials, mine was filled with scrolls from back to front. The scrolls had gold letters written on each. He made me understand that because I had obeyed Him and suffered for His cause all my life, my reward and mission were greater than that of the others I saw by the will of the Father. I also understood that even though He loves everyone the same because He is the Great and righteous Judge, He gives rewards according to faithfulness.

The scriptures say in Romans 2:6-7 that Jesus will judge everyone according to their actions. He will give eternal life to those who keep on doing good, seeking after the glory, honor, and immortality that God offers. And 1 Corinthians. 3:8 makes a statement that although we are all one in the work of the Lord, as some plant and other water, nonetheless, each will receive his reward according to his labor.

SCROLLS OF DESTINY

The following scripture speaks about a little scroll, and it reminds me of what I saw in my heavenly drawer:

"So, I went to the angel and told him to give me the little scroll. And he said to me, "Take and eat it; it will make your stomach bitter, but in your mouth, it will be sweet as honey." And I took the little scroll from the hand of the angel and ate it." (Revelation 10:9–10 ESV)

When I saw them, I told Jesus, "Wow! Jesus! What is this?"

Jesus told me, "This is yours, and it has to do with your destiny. They are here until the time comes in which you will claim it, and it will be given to you."

"But what are they?" I asked Him, very puzzled.

Jesus told me, "These are *songs* of the Father about you."

Then I said, "What? The Father sings?"

Jesus lovingly responded, "Who created music?"

I answered, astounded, with a sigh, 'The Father!'"

Suddenly, I understood and realized that if the Father was the One who created music and worship, then He must be the best singer in the world!

I must confess that if I had read this scripture before this revelation, I would not remember it. But after this revelation, as I delved into the scriptures to get my revelation clearer in light of them, I came across a passage that has amazed me ever since. It is Zephaniah 3:17, and here it is in three different translations:

The Lord, your God, is with you; His power gives you victory. The Lord will take delight in you, and in His love, He will give you new life. He will sing and be joyful over you. (GNT)

He will quiet you with his love and exalt over you with loud singing. (ESV)

With his love, he will calm all your fears. He will rejoice over you with joyful songs. (NLT)

SONGS OF THE FATHER

To continue the revelation, Jesus told me, "Every time you obey me and suffer for my cause, the Father sings a new song about you. The angels take that song, write it in a scroll with golden letters, and put it in this drawer."

I thought to myself, *About me?* I felt unworthy, but at the same time, I was astonished by His love for me. I had never felt so loved! In Proverbs 8:17, God tells us He loves those who love Him, and those who seek Him diligently will find Him. John

12:25-26 also gives us a picture of what it means to love God more profoundly, even to the point of losing everything, but in the end, the Father will honor us. It says, "If you love your life, you will lose it. If you give it up in this world, you will be given eternal life. If you serve me, you must go with me. My servants will be with me wherever I am. If you serve me, my Father will honor you" (CEV).

Then suddenly, I saw a worship leader standing to the side, waiting for something. "Give it to him," Jesus said as he grabbed a scroll from the drawer and handed it to me.

So, I took it and handed it on to him. As soon as I handed it to him He flew to several Nations of the world. As he walked away, I could see the Nations he was going to in the background.

Jesus made it clear to me that this worshiper was one of many to whom I had to deliver these scrolls for them to be carried to every corner of the earth.

"Why are you providing this to this worshiper?" I inquired of Jesus.?"

Jesus told me, "I choose worshipers who live a life of obedience and holiness."

He immediately revealed to me that He selects worshipers who maintain holiness and faithful obedience to Him. I also realized that Jesus would raise many more of these worshipers who would bring the Father's songs to every corner of the earth because the Father seeks such worshipers for the last days' revival.

Then at that moment, He looked at me closer and told me the most astonishing words I've ever heard, so deep and hard to understand humanly. He told me, "I am about to give you something so big that it will go around the world, something that I did not even give to King David."

When He told me this, I thought of worship and immediately asked Him, "Could it be possible that worship can bring revival?"

Jesus answered, "I dwell, and I am enthroned in the worship of the righteous."

I now feel that this was a mystery revealed to us in Psalm 22:3, but many have missed it or did not have a more profound revelation of what this meant, especially for the last days. I could not understand it entirely until Jesus told me those words, and I read them in the scriptures. He is truly enthroned upon our praises. He inhabits and sits in the midst of the most beautiful worship of the redeemed, His beloved bride—the church. When we take our focus off earthly things and focus on Him, we are indeed able to honor Him by giving Him the place He deserves in our hearts and minds. He takes total control, and He can manifest with all His glory as described in this scripture, "Yet You are holy, O You who are enthroned upon [or You who inhabits] the praises of Israel" (Psalm 22:3 NASB). [emphasis mine]

THE POWER OF WORSHIP

Jesus gave me insight that when His people worship and praise Him, He becomes our hiding place, shields us from our enemies, and surrounds us with powerful songs of deliverance (see Psalm 32:7). When this happens, souls are set free, and saved, healed, and transformed; therefore, resulting to the revival of souls.

My eyes were immediately opened. I began to see that many worshipers were being raised, and their worship would win the spiritual realm, releasing a river of healing, miracles, deliverance, and salvation. More specifically, I saw God Himself inhabiting and dwelling with transforming power in the midst of His people's worship. He then continued by telling me, "You will convey the songs of the Father to the world, and His breath and word will be sung to all nations. This will release the Father's Lordship on Earth."

Indeed, you and I must sing the Father's Breath and His word to the nations. Oh yes, we must "sing for joy to the Lord, all the earth; [and] praise him with songs and shouts of joy! [We must] sing praises to the Lord" and play musical instruments for him (Psalm 98:4–5 GNT). [emphasis mine]

We must sing His praise from the ends of the earth. We must sing to the Lord a new song that has never been heard before because it comes from the breath of God in a new way. The time has come when all the former things have come to pass, and we must now declare new things with God (see Isaiah 42:9–14).

In my revelation, I started telling the Lord, "But Lord, how is that going to happen? I am so limited in the piano, and when I try writing a new song, I get frustrated because I won't go past a certain level, and I just give up and go."

Jesus said to me, "I was ready to give it to you every time you reached that point of frustration, when it seemed like a dead end, but you gave up and left, so I couldn't. When you are in the place where you feel like giving up it is at the point when I will give it to you if you press in until it is given to you.

Then He told me, "You must go, take my worship, and raise more worshipers, and from these scrolls, you will give to many more until the world is filled with the songs of the Father to the point that the worship of the Father is greater than the worship of the devil on earth,"

I always thought that God had more worshipers on earth than the devil, but when Jesus told me this, I was surprised to find it out. I've come to a new understanding that authentic, spirit-led worship is rare even within the church. This realization underscores the significance of the Father seeking worshipers who will genuinely worship in spirit and truth, especially as we approach the last days. (see John 4:23-24)

God created us to declare His praise, and as we testify through our worship, there will be more and more worshipers who will give glory to God, just as proclaimed by the following scriptures:

"All of this is for your benefit, and as God's grace reaches more and more people, there will be great thanksgiving, and God will receive more and more glory" (2 Corinthians 4:15).

"After this I saw a vast crowd, too great to count, from every nation and tribe and people and language, standing in front of the throne and before the Lamb. They were clothed in white robes and held palm branches in their hands. And they were shouting with a great roar, "Salvation comes from our God who sits on the throne and from the Lamb!"" (Revelation 7:9–10, NLT)

Continuing with my revelation, when Jesus told me this, I replied, "But Lord, when will this take place? How am I going to claim and get those scrolls? How will that be if I have so many other limitations?"

I told Him this because I perceived it as challenging and difficult, given the struggles I was experiencing at that time However, Jesus said,

"Everything is okay in me. You humans add the limitations, but in me, there are no limitations. In me, all is well."

UNITED WITH JESUS

While He was speaking these words to me, I felt as though my very essence—whether it was my body or spirit, I cannot say for certain—merged into Jesus, becoming one with Him, then I came back out again. This experience transcended a mere physical phenomenon; it was a deep, spiritual union. During this union with Jesus, I was enveloped by a profound peace and sweetness, and I felt a powerful force strengthening me in a supernatural way. The experience radiated overwhelming tenderness, love, and a peace so profound that human words fall short of capturing it. I could feel it with every fiber of my being, experiencing the reality of Jesus' assurance that indeed, 'everything is perfectly okay within Him.

Now I understand that He was speaking in my language so I could understand. He was telling me that everything is completely correct and well in Him; everything is perfectly good within Him for He is the truth. There is nothing corrupt or twisted in Him; I could trust Him blindly and, therefore, there are no limitations to His goodness, everything is possible if I could believe that He was trustworthy.

These words unleashed in me an intimate moment filled with a new revelation about who Jesus is. I felt astonished by this new revelation. Now I deeply understand what the Psalmist says in Psalm 92:15:

"Lord is just! He is my rock! There is no evil [or wickedness] in him!." [emphasis mine]

I now understand better when the scripture says, "But he who is joined to the Lord becomes one spirit with Him." (1 Corinthians 6:17, ESV).

I find the words Jesus said to me very interesting. He told me that humans are the ones that put limitations on Him, but that inside of Him, all is perfect. This made me understand that I had nothing to worry about since all is possible if we truly believe in who He is—His character, holiness, faithfulness, integrity, love, and power. As Jesus told His disciples in Mark 10:27, with man, it was impossible, but not with God. All things are possible, and nothing is impossible with God when we blindly believe in Him (also see Luke 1:37).

I also understood from this moment when I went inside of

Jesus and became one with Him that this is how I can experience Philippians 4:13, which describes that I can do all things through Him who strengthens me. This also leads me to Hebrews 11:6, which clearly teaches me that without that kind of trust and faith, it is impossible to please Him. No wonder He is with me, and His power gives me victory. The Lord takes delight in me and gives me life in His love. The Father delights with great joy and sings over you and me (see Zephaniah 3:17).

BEFORE THE FATHER'S THRONE

Continuing with the revelation, Jesus took me by the hand, and we left that place. He said, "Come, I will take you to the throne of my Father."

I was overwhelmed with gratitude while trembling in awe. Then we stood in front of the seven lamps (the seven spirits of God) and the river that flowed from the Father's throne. When I looked, I was amazed, thinking to myself, *Wow! The Father loves me!* The love of the Father became so real to me at that moment. It was a new revelation to me of His inexplicable love. I was standing before the Author of love, who loved me so profoundly.

While standing there, all I could see was something resembling a golden crown adorned with precious stones, with the likeness of a throne set against a backdrop of brilliant white light emanating from the throne.

Now I understand more deeply what Jesus meant when He said that *all things had been handed over to Him by the Father. No one sees Jesus except through the Father, and no one sees the Father except through Jesus and anyone to whom Jesus chooses to reveal him to* (see Matthew 11:27). This was a significant moment where Jesus chose to reveal the Father to me. In John 14:21, Jesus reminds me that His Father will love those who love His Son and that Jesus will also love me *and* reveal Himself to me (see John 14:20–21). I feel so inspired as these words permeate my Spirit. I love You, Jesus!

In the revelation, there, before the Father's throne room, I felt such profound love from the Father. There was an inexplicable peace that I had never felt before nor after in my life on this earth. As I was looking, I told Jesus in awe, "The Father sings about me?" I sighed as I said, "*Wow!* The Father *loves* me!" as I was taking in and processing this overwhelming truth about God the Father. The Lord knew I needed this fresh revelation of His love because, at that time, I was going through a very hard time. But there, His presence was so fragrant and sweet and was profoundly ministering to my heart.

Jesus says in His word that if I love Him and keep His word, His Father will love me, and *They* will come to me and make *Their* home with me. Jesus also says in the scriptures that His Father sent His Holy Spirit in Jesus' name to teach me all things and bring to my remembrance all that Jesus said. He also continues in the same passage of scripture, saying that He will leave us a gift—peace of mind and heart—that the world cannot give us. (See John 14:23–27)

I honestly experienced that peace for the first time in my life in the purest and holiest way ever when standing before God's throne. In John 17, Jesus had a very intimate conversation with the Father about you and me where He asked the Father that you and I (His disciples) may be one, just as the Father is in Jesus and Jesus is in the Father, so that we (you and I) may also be in *Them*, and in this way the world will acknowledge that the Father sent Jesus.

One thing I noticed was that the Father did not talk to me because Jesus was talking to me, and it was as if the Father was talking to me through Jesus. I also noticed that time in heaven was different. It was as if time did not exist. It felt as if everything happened simultaneously within eternity in heaven. There was no way to measure time in heaven since there is no such thing as the limitation of time. At times, it seemed as if Jesus spoke to me without words, transmitting revelation and knowledge just by being with Him. Other times He would talk to me, and His voice would penetrate my soul and make me tremble. I must admit, this experience is very difficult to explain in human words, so I am doing my best to explain It, but it's challenging.

MY HOME IN HEAVEN

Then Jesus took my hand again and told me, "I am going to show you something." And as we walked, I would look at Him, and I was in awe that He was holding my hand. He would smile at me and talk to me as a down-to-earth person and intimate friend. Then we went into this place, which looked like a living room of a house made of gold, and I asked Him, "What is this?"

He told me, "This is going to be your house." I was amazed because the whole house was made of gold and was beautiful, and even though I only saw the living room, I could see that there were many more rooms in that house because it was big.

Jesus told me, "Each time you obey me and suffer for my cause, this house becomes bigger and more beautiful." I was astonished but excited. I felt so loved by Jesus, and I realized that everything I had suffered for Him, which was a lot, was worth it after all. Jesus knew that this would minister to my heart because I had just lost my earthly house for the sake of the ministry and was still grieving it.

Jesus knows what it is to learn obedience through what He suffered. And through that suffering, He was made perfect to become the source of our eternal salvation if we obey Him.

Jesus modeled humility by becoming obedient to the point of death—and a ruthless one, at that—yet this was what brought us our salvation opportunity (see Philippians 2:8).

So, I have come to understand now how obedience, even to the point of suffering or death, is so important in the life of a true worshiper (see Hebrews 5:8–9). When we understand this, we rejoice in our sufferings, knowing that suffering produces endurance in our relationship with God. This endurance produces a godly character in us, and this godly character produces in us a hope for our future, and this hope never puts us to shame because the Holy Spirit pours God's love into our hearts (see Romans 5:3–5 and 2 Corinthians 1:5)

Jesus also told me that I should not let my heart be distressed but instead believe in Him. When Jesus showed me my house, He also reminded me of what He said in John 14. He said that there are many dwelling places in His Father's house and that He goes ahead of us to prepare a place. This is because He wants us to be with Him. God is so good to us; He wants our company eternally.

When we left the house, I found myself with Jesus again by the river that came out of the throne. As I held His hand, I reflected and contemplated everything He had revealed to me in awe. I started saying to Him, "Jesus, I don't want to go. I want to stay with You here."

But Jesus gave me a sweet smile and said, "You must go and accomplish this great mission that the Father has given you," As He was saying these words, my hands started to slip away from His hands. I started going down as He was looking at me with a warm look filled with love, and in loving words, He told me, "I can't wait until you can be with me here again!"

BACK TO EARTH

Suddenly, I was aware of my surroundings as I heard my husband, Herman, speaking through the microphone, announcing that we would pray for the children because the children needed to be part of this as well. I realized that I had just come back from a heavenly revelation. I could hardly walk because I felt the heaviness of heaven on and in me. A woman from the congregation sister Daisy, who was present that night, looked at me to help me get up, and I told her, "I have just come from heaven." She laughed and thought I was kidding, so I repeated it to her. This time she was puzzled, but I could hardly speak. That night I told my experience to a few people who stayed wondering what had happened to me. I went home that night with a divine impartation that words cannot explain. My husband had to hold me to take me to the car and out from it into our house.

The next day was Sunday, and as I was leading worship, the presence of God was supernaturally stronger than usual. I felt the Spirit of God impress on me a new song, and I could hear the Spirit telling me to sing the song of the Father. As I started singing the song of the Father prophetically and spontaneously, the following song came forth:

Be holy because I am holy, I seek holiness in you, I am holy, holy, holy...

I repeated this several times. As I was releasing the song of the Father, two ladies from our church were being delivered, one from a suicide spirit and the other from a homicide spirit; both were new converts.

The song of the Lord released the Spirit of holiness and power, bringing spiritual deliverance and freedom! Praise God! Ever since this experience of heaven; I have had two whirlwinds of fire, one on each of my sides. At times it intensifies and starts to burn all around my neck, both of my arms, chest, and back. They are constantly there, even though at times they tame down, but then at times, they intensify again. My life has never been the same after that. The Lord was giving me a new song every month. Just like Jesus said, if I pressed in and did not give up, He would give me the Father's songs. I praise You, Father, for Your goodness and greatness!

Indeed, the Father surrounds you and me with songs of deliverance through His loving breath. This is an amazing gem of truth, something to ponder on deeply (see Psalm 32:7). Not only are we delivered by His mighty love, but He promises that if you and I overcome, He will grant you and me the right to sit with Him on His throne, as He sat down with His Father on His throne after He conquered (see Revelation 3:21).

As I continue studying the Word, I find more gems that clarify this heavenly revelation. The following scripture clarifies my experience with Jesus: "I have used parables to tell you these things, the time will come when I will not use parables but will speak to you plainly about the Father. When that day comes, you will ask him in my name; and I do not say that I will ask him on your behalf, for the Father himself loves you. He loves you because you love me and have believed that I came from God." (John 16:25–27 GNT)

We, the Bride of Christ, must bless the Lord at all times. You and I need to have His Praise in our mouths continually. Our soul needs to boast in the Lord. We must magnify the Lord and exalt His name in humility and glad heart (see Psalm 34:1–3). You and I need to glorify His name with trembling fear, for He is holy. As we worship the King of kings and Lord of Lords, all nations will follow us and praise Him for His righteous acts that have been revealed (see Revelation 15:4).

PURSUING GOD'S COMMISSION

All of these—my childhood dreams, college preparation,

trials and difficulties, many prophetic words, and finally, my revelation of heaven—culminated in starting a worship school in 2011 called Selah. I started giving prophetic worship training seminars and later traveled to other churches doing a series of training lasting up to twelve weeks.

Some pastors started asking for my help with their worship teams, which was part of God's mandate to raise worshipers for His glory. This book is part of the answer to this need. It has not been an easy mandate. God allowed some things to happen in my life throughout the course of writing this book so that you can be blessed by it. I went through some valleys and hard times through this journey. I received many attacks from the enemy, but God helped me overcome them. The enemy will fight the true worship of our God, but remember, the One in us is greater than the one in the world.

My mission in writing this book is to influence a new generation of worshipers and revivalists who pursue an intimate relationship with God —to raise intimate worship generals, worshipers who don't just sing about revival but instead are revived. The Father's desire is to raise worshipers who would come out of the threshing floor of God pure, cleansed, sanctified, humble, selfless, mature, useful servants, focused on Jesus, lovers of God, intimates of God, and living as fragrant sacrifices to the Almighty Omnipotent God!

My mandate from the Father is: "You must go and take my worship and raise worshipers, and from these scrolls, you will give to many more until the world is filled with the songs of the Father, and the worship to the Father would be more than worship to the devil on earth. Go and take my songs and breath to the nations."

This is why the Apostle says in 2 Corinthians 4:15 that *all* of this is for your benefit. And as God's grace reaches *more* and *more* people, there will be great thanksgiving, and God will receive *more* and *more* glory. God formed you and me to declare His praise.

Take a minute right now and make a declaration of praise to the Lord! He is worthy of your praise. (see Isaiah 43:21) Let's fill the earth with the songs of the Father! Keep pressing in no matter what!

A NEW SONG

A year after this revelation, in 2010, the Lord allowed me to record an album called, *The Father's Songs*. I will tell you how the title of the song, "The Father's Songs," was birthed.

I asked the Lord to give me a new song that had to do with my experience in heaven so that His people would get a new revelation of His love for them. It didn't seem like I was getting anywhere for a few days. Then, one night, I dimmed the lights in my Holy Spirit room, turned on my piano, and began worshiping the Father with all my heart and soul until about 2:00 am.

Suddenly, I saw in the Spirit that an angel had arrived at my left side, and in his hands, he had a scroll identical to the ones that Jesus showed me in the revelation of heaven. The angel was looking at me as he went on to open the scroll.

At first, I thought to myself, *Oh, great; God is going to give me that new song now*. But it wasn't happening. I saw the angel with the opened scroll as if he was waiting for a command. I was getting frustrated because it was about 4:00 am, and it still was not happening. Then, the Holy Spirit reminded me of what Jesus had told me in heaven, "When you are in the place where you feel like giving up, it is at that point that I will give it to you *if* you continue to press on without giving up."

I, however, was exhausted, so I said, 'Jesus, I am very tired. I'll be back tomorrow to continue.' Then, I went to sleep. I had two dreams when I was sleeping, one after the other. In one dream, I heard a heavenly symphony playing the most exuberant music I've ever heard. This must have been a huge symphony because I could hear all sorts of instruments and melodies that were *not* earthly. I could not even keep up with the melodies that were so richly and beautifully coming out of this symphony.

Then, I had another dream right after this one where I was singing a new song. It was *so* beautiful! While dreaming this, I remember saying to myself, "I want to wake up to write these melodies down before I forget them."

When I woke up, the only word I could remember from the whole song was "Victory." I could not remember any of the melodies I heard in the dream after I woke up. But when I woke up that next day, I returned and kept pressing in with even more persistence and enthusiasm. In fact, I kept at it until the Lord finally released the new song to me at 4:48 pm on May 26, 2010. Praise God because He is good and merciful all the time!

I sang this song for the first time in public at my church the Sunday after this, and as I was singing, I heard some very celestial sounds that I'd never heard played before on any earthly instrument. I can't even identify exactly what instrument was playing, as I was playing the piano and singing. It was sort of like a high-timbre sound, a beautifully harmonizing sound! I was the only one playing (and the drummer was hardly playing because it was a new song for him).

Then, after the service, one of the worshipers told me that her eyes were supernaturally opened when I was singing that song, and she saw a very tall angel behind me. And when she looked around the church, there were angels all around the church singing this song with me. I became very excited and understood the entire reason for the heavenly sounds I had heard; the angels were present, playing the Father's song with me.

A few days before the recording of the album, the Lord spoke to me through a friend's dream where she saw a huge angel that was over the church where this recording took place. She asked him if he was there to sing, and the angel told her he was there to guard the place during the recording. Then, she saw 134 more angels coming to the recording to sing with me. She told me that this recording was by the Father's will and approval and that He was with me in this project. This was a very timely word I needed to hear at the moment.

During this recording, healing and spiritual deliverance took place, and the heavens were opened over the entire place. I prayed that this recording would touch people's hearts, bring them into the holy of holies, and release a new revelation of the Father's love over them. Even after ten years, I keep hearing testimonials about the many people this album has ministered to around the world. I have received social media messages and emails from people who have encountered God through this album.

So, I say again, *keep pressing in.* God is never late.

Chapter 4

His Presence is Our Origin

The word of God, His breath, is a fountain of life in my soul. His breath is in us. His *breath* in us connects us to that place where we originated from—His presence. His presence is home to our Spirit. We were created to be intimate worshipers of the King. As Saint Augustine said, "You made us for Yourself, and our hearts are restless until they rest in thee."[1]

I have realized that worship is more powerful than many understand or even believe it to be. Worship is more than simply singing or playing an instrument. Worship is an attitude of the heart that acknowledges who He is. It is a deliberate refocusing of our minds and hearts on Him, proclaiming His names and attributes into the atmospheres around us daily. It is also surrendering everything, living a life worthy of Him, and living for Him, not for ourselves.

In Mark 12:30, Jesus tells us that, as worshipers, we are to love the Lord God with all our hearts, soul, mind, and strength. I also believe that when we actively worship with our voices, hands, or bodies in the way that John 4:23-24 instructs, we are directly connected to our divine origin, His presence, at the highest levels ever—a level of holy intimate communion with God.

I love to worship God with a new song every day, one that is prophetic and spontaneous and comes directly from my relationship with Him. I believe worship is the answer to many problems in life. It brings my attention back to what matters most—my relationship with my Creator. It reconnects me with God, the source of my life.

During these periods of intense, intimate worship, I have received more revelation of God—His character, divine nature, and power. It's like being permeated by the Holy Spirit, who reveals God's secrets to my Spirit. God has spoken His secrets and mysteries into my ears as I surrender to Him without a religious spirit and without fear of man. With this, I mean to break away from the intimidating religious mindset or fear of what others might think, and to take my worship into the spiritual realm where many dare not enter. During these times of intimate, deeper, genuine, and non-rushed worship, I have received a deeper understanding of His love and grace for me.

I'll give you an example. One day, as I was worshiping God and pouring my whole self into Him in worship and honor, my eyes were opened. I saw His throne by revelation. I could not see Him, but I could see a very bright light coming from His throne. It made me think of a painting which depicts the white throne with the 24 elders and the four living things surrounding it. It was as if that picture had become a reality to me. All this happened as I sang a new song in the Spirit, completely surrendering myself in worship to Him.

Then He took me back to creation when He created the first human being. He took me to Gen. 2:7 (ESV), "Then the Lord God formed man from the dust of the ground and breathed into his nostrils the breath [or spirit] of life, and the man became a living being."

I realized that while the man was just lying there, he was just dust (like clay), and he was not a living being, but the minute that the mighty God breathed His breath into Adam's nostrils, then he became a living soul.

I felt impressed by God asking me, *Where did this breath come from?*

Then He showed me the day I was created. I could see how I came to be a living soul. I came right from the "gut" of His mighty presence, His divine "self," through His breath! My Spirit came from that mighty throne! That's when I realized that my origin was not from Puerto Rico or my parents but from His mighty presence. I originated as a living being in his presence and was later formed in my mother's womb. I was overwhelmed and amazed by this discovery. This was the most intimate and warm thought I'd ever had. I felt so close to Him, like never before.

I realized that we were created in the midst of the beauty and splendor of God's majesty. We were created in the midst of angels, numbering myriads of myriads and thousands of thousands, in the midst of the four living creatures and the 24 elders, right in the majestic throne of the *Most High*, in the midst of the Trinity's heart—the Father, Son, and Holy Spirit! Our origin is based on beauty, splendor, and love in the purest form ever known. My life has never been the same after this experience.

More understanding came regarding this experience as time passed. All this happened while I was singing a new song spontaneously, intimately pouring my soul into Him, abandoning, and surrendering myself to Him in the most powerful worship that could exist: In Spirit and truth.

Do you want to get deeper into Him and know His secrets and mysteries? Have you ever felt the sweet presence of God? Have you noticed how your Spirit feels at home there? Have you noticed how your Spirit wants to stay there and never leave that sweet and peaceful place? It is because the presence of God is home to our human Spirit, our origin, where our human Spirit originated. Because our spirits originated from His mighty Self, His Spirit is our fiercely jealous lover who desires our Spirit to return to Him. He is a jealous God because we belong to Him.

Every time I read the following scripture, I tremble in awe of how God has planned every detail of my life. It amazes me and gives me this sense of security because all is good in Him, and He controls every detail of my life and future. As it says in Jeremiah 1:5 (ESV), "Before I formed you in the womb I knew you, before you were born, I consecrated you; I appointed you a prophet to the nations."

Then Psalm 139:13–18 (NKJV) gives a more detailed enumeration of how He designed and planned me, how He loves and cares for me until this day:

For You formed my inward parts; You covered me in my mother's womb. I will praise You, for I am fearfully and wonderfully made; marvelous are Your works, and that my soul knows very well. My frame was not hidden from You, when I was made in secret, and skillfully wrought in the lowest parts of the earth. Your eyes saw my substance, being yet unformed. And in Your book, they all were written, the days fashioned for me, when as yet there were none of them. How precious also are Your thoughts to me, O God! How great is the sum of them! If I should count them, they would be more in number than the sand; when I awake, I am still with You.

This last verse especially deeply warms my heart. I like how the New Living Translation says this phrase: "And when I wake up, you are still with me!"

To know that after all these years, when I wake up, He is

still with me, just as from day one of my creation, is an intimate feeling of indescribable love.

The following Is an excerpt from one of my journals about my encounters with Him:

- Your presence is where I belong. In Your presence, I find my song,
- Where my journey first came to be. You are my Home, where I feel so free.
- My soul and Spirit, they very well know, the place where love and grace do flow.
- As we walk, hand in hand, my Guide, in Your presence, all else cast aside.
- When together, our hearts take flight, nothing's missing, all feels so right.
- Like lovers' stroll in a heavenly dream, heaven and I, in harmony, gleam.
- In the night, love songs I sing to You, my soul flows in the wine of Your presence.
- With You, I'm sheltered, completely protected, in Your embrace, my heart's always connected.
- In Your presence, I find my song, in Your presence, is where I belong.
- My origin, my eternal destiny in your grace, oh, how I await for our divine embrace!

Chapter 5

Created to Bring God Glory

Doctor Cindy Trimm once said, "Worship is in your DNA. When you were created, you were created with worship embedded in your DNA. So, you are always engaged in worship whether you know it or not–whether to God or to whom/what He created. Every morning, direct your focus to God; it should be your honor and responsibility to do so!"[1]

I was created to bring glory to God and to worship Him eternally, and so were you (see Isaiah 43:1–7). As Ruth Ward Heflin said, "Praise until the Spirit of worship comes. Worship until the glory comes. Then stand in the glory!" I would add to this, stand, *and stay* in the glorious presence of the lovely King.

Worship is not a song service. Worship is the language of heaven. We must worship because it is the eternal purpose of our lives. I have found so much revelation during my worship that it has radically transformed how I see and live life and the way I understand eternity. True worship has caused a paradigm shift in my life. As Psalm 104:1–2 says, "Let all that I am praise the LORD. O LORD my God, how great you are! You are robed with honor and majesty. You are dressed in a robe of light..."

My heart is constantly filled with gratitude toward God. I find myself constantly saying things like, "Thank you, Jesus! How beautiful You are! You are so good! Thank You for Your love. I love You so much, Jesus. You are the King of my life."

I was not always like this, but when I discovered the secret of worship, it changed everything. I became a different person, free from religiosity and able to be an intimate friend of God. This is not instant; it requires intentionality. It involves your whole mind, heart, body, and strength, just like any meaningful relationship. This is the most precious relationship we'll ever have. It is an eternal, intimate relationship with our Originator and Creator. This is why the Father seeks worshipers who worship Him in Spirit and truth.

I discovered that every time I truly worship God from my heart (in Spirit and truth), His powerful Presence would become so profoundly evident in me and around me that I would feel like I was walking in a glorious cloud. I felt high in the air. I felt light like a feather, and all my burdens would lift away from me. I felt so drunk in His love that it was much easier to love those who did not love me.

Worship is so powerful it can transform your lifestyle. It helps you overcome the difficulties you face effortlessly because you are just riding the waves with Him as the Victor. The worship of the redeemed has so much power that it can even conquer cities and nations. Consider the prevalent secular music and how some of the most demonic music has swept across many countries and profoundly altered their local culture. How much more power would the true worship of the redeemed of Christ have?

When we truly worship God from the heart and in Spirit, we can become the channels through which the heavens open to transform cities and nations for Him. We become conduits for His powerful presence. When the presence of God touches a city, demons flee, and things cannot stay the same any longer. It's like lighting a city on fire. It all starts small, then speeds up radically fast until it's uncontrollable. Spirit-led worship can do the same. This true worship that can spark revival is not your typical song service. It is a surrendered, no-agenda, no-program, and not-rushed kind of worship. Remember that this is the type of lifestyle of worship that God our Father wants.

One day preaching, teaching, and church services will end, but worship to the Father will never end. We were created to worship. We were not created to be enslaved by time and programs, slogans, and events; we were created to worship eternally without haste and time limitations. That's who we are—eternal worshipers of the Father. Isn't this the true purpose of the Bible? That we become true worshipers of God? This is not just for musicians or singers. The word of God is supposed to teach ALL of us to be true worshipers in every sense of the word because God is that worthy! To worship the Origin of our existence is our eternal purpose!

If you want revival, it will cost you everything. Since 2009, I've had the dream that one day, every restaurant, shop, mall, business, doctor's office, lawyer's office, and even federal and state offices will play prophetic, spontaneous, and Spirit-led worship and that people will experience and see the glory of God manifested at each of these places.

I know what you are thinking. It sounds like a crazy idea and one that will never happen. Well, I always have wild dreams about this and other things with the Father. But do you really believe that God cannot fulfill this? I believe that when it is right, He will.

Everyone worships every day. If you don't worship God, then you are definitely worshiping a person or a thing or even yourself. The word of God mandates that You and I must not have any other god but Him; this includes our ministry, church, business, talents, or personal agendas. God mandates that we must not make for ourselves an idol of any kind or an image of anything in the heavens, on the earth, or in the sea. The Lord, our God, is a jealous God, and He will not tolerate our affection for any other gods. (see Exodus 20:3–5).

Chapter 6

Called to be a Prophetic Worshiper

First, why do I use the term *prophetic worship*? I understand that this concept scares some brethren but bear with me for a moment. If there is anyone that is careful about the prophetic, it is me. I had many bad experiences with so-called prophets who would either prophesy falsely or misuse and abuse the prophetic. I understand that kind of abuse and misuse of the gift firsthand.Although I must say I've also seen this and other types of abuse throughout the years in the offices of pastors, evangelists, missionaries, teachers, politicians, etc.

However, when I refer to prophetic worship, I am speaking about a different kind of worship, a worship that comes from the Spirit-led intimate place. This is a worship that is alive and spontaneous, with a new anointed sound emanating from the tones of the throne of God that brings life from the Spirit. This level of worship ushers in the presence of God even before the mouth is open. It is a worship that flows from the river of the throne and releases the resurrection power through the Holy Spirit. It is a worship that opens a heavenly atmosphere where there is revelation, empowerment, freedom, deliverance, divine guidance, transformation, salvation, restoration, and healing. This worship touches the body, mind, soul, and spirit. It is the kind of worship that releases the kingdom of God, as witnessed by the 24 elders and the four living creatures around the throne. It releases the tones of the throne into our earthly atmosphere, facilitating the manifestation of the holy glory of God within us.

Prophetic worship is the highest level of musical worship in the universe because it comes from the redeemed by the blood of the Lamb. It becomes a new song of the heart that no one knows except the redeemed. You cannot call this level of worship a song service or a usual worship song. Hence, I call it prophetic and intimate worship.

This type of worship takes a high level of commitment to God; since it is worship with a holy fire of God's glory, we need to treat it with fear of God and reverence. More about this later in the book.

ALL ARE CALLED TO WORSHIP THE LORD

From this book first edition I have made some revisions regarding this topic to bring clarity to this chapter's goal. Throughout my experience in ministry, I've observed a common enthusiasm for singing and playing instruments within a church context. However, many seem to miss an important understanding: we are called to worship and minister **first** unto the Lord in the secret place before anything else. (see 2 Chronicles 29:11) This calling demands a higher level of commitment and responsibility before God. It is, indeed, the most powerful form of ministry, one that never ends.

In every aspect of our lives, each of us embodies some form of leadership, guiding and influencing those around us in various capacities. However, in the specific context of spiritual leadership within a church setting, the role transcends beyond mere performance. Leading people into God's presence demands significant responsibilities and a deep commitment before God that encompasses more than just singing or playing an instrument. Spiritual leadership, in this sense, involves inspiring and guiding others towards a deeper revelation and connection with God, nurturing their faith, and exemplifying the values and teachings of the word of God.

Developing Musical Proficiency is a foundation in the music-worship ministry. This doesn't necessarily mean professional-level skills, but at least a basic proficiency in singing, playing an instrument, or other forms of musical expression is important. If you're in the early stages of your musical journey, it's beneficial to focus on learning and practicing these skills. Remember, the pulpit isn't a place for initial music training; it's where refined skills are utilized to be able to lead worship effectively.

Worship can be led in many ways beyond singing or playing an instrument. If these aren't your strengths, consider other avenues like prophetic dance, sound engineering, or technology. These roles also require skill and training but offer alternative pathways to participate in the worship ministry.

UNDERSTANDING THE HEART OF WORSHIP

True worship leadership goes beyond musical ability. It involves a deep, personal devotion and understanding of worship's purpose. Leading worship is about guiding others into a spiritual experience, which requires a leader to be deeply connected and committed to their own spiritual journey with God. If your primary interest lies solely in the musical aspect, it would be worthwhile to explore and deepen your understanding of the broader spiritual meaning of worship according to the Scriptures."

Being called to pulpit worship ministry is a combination of natural talent, spiritual anointing, and the desire for continual growth and learning. Here are three indicators that you might be called to this ministry:

1. Natural Talent: Often, those called to music-worship ministry have a natural inclination towards music from a young age, noticeable not only to themselves but also to others around them, including people beyond their immediate circle.
2. Spiritual Anointing: A key indicator of a calling to music-worship ministry is that your song or instrument carries the presence of God stemming from the secret intimate place. As you minister unto the Lord, this intimacy ushers God's presence into the congregation, thereby creating a profound spiritual impact in people's lives.
3. Relentless Commitment to Growth: God equips those He calls. If you find yourself eager to learn, improve, and embrace training in both your musical skills and spiritual leadership, this is a strong indication of your calling. This journey should feel enriching and driven by a deep passion for true worship and spiritual leadership.

If you feel called to pulpit worship ministry, begin by assessing your musical skills and exploring various forms of worship leadership. It's important to deepen your spiritual understanding of worship through the scriptures and commit to continual learning. By doing so, you'll be well-equipped to lead others effectively in worship. You will not only guide them into the glorious presence of God but also empower them to do the same.

PRACTICE THE HEART AND SKILL OF WORSHIP

The worship ministry is not a Hollywood opportunity to make you famous or popular. It is a place to make *Jesus* famous and exalt *Him* only.

When you are called to the altar ministry of worship, perhaps you are not at the level you would love to be. Nonetheless, others notice that you are a fast learner and are in continuous, stable, and notable growth in your instrument.

This ministry comes with a high price: the sacrifice of continually dying to oneself. Yes, it is a great privilege, but it carries an even higher responsibility. Whether we are called to be a pulpit worship leader or not, we are all called to worship God, as we were created for this very purpose. Your worship is not determined by, nor dependent on, your position in the ministry. There are many other powerful and awe-inspiring ministries in the Kingdom of God. In these, God can use you even more effectively to make a difference in people's lives—especially if that is your true calling from the Lord. In these ministries too, you serve with a heart full of worship. God has placed gifts and talents in you since birth. It's important to explore and discover what they are to become more effective in the Kingdom of God. Some people prefer to be servants, assisting the worship ministry in various ways, which is completely fine. Remember, Levites are servants first.

I understand that some churches don't have a worship team due to a lack of proficient musicians or singers, or perhaps because those available are not fully committed. Nonetheless, I am thankful for resources like Spotify, iTunes, and YouTube worship. These can be excellent interim solutions until you train a team, or if you lack musicians. Using these resources for great worship is perfectly acceptable to facilitate congregational worship. The repeat button is always there to let a song flow when the Spirit moves.

Remember, a song in itself is not worship; worship comes from the heart. It's not about the resource but the hearts of the redeemed. The resource is merely a means. Sometimes, it can be better, as those musicians won't interrupt the flow, especially if you choose the right worship songs beforehand or have good playlists ready.

If you wish to serve in the worship ministry, seek God's presence in prayer. Ask Him to reveal the ministry He wants you involved in, one for which He has already equipped you. Be aware of the difference between aspiring to something and being called to it. Ask God what He has in His heart for you. I assure you; He will reveal it.

Scriptures recount that Kenaniah, the head Levite, was chosen as choir leader for his skill (1 Chronicles 15:22–27). From King David's worship order, we learn about the 288 accomplished musicians. They were trained by their fathers and played cymbals, harps, and lyres at the house of God. The primary worship leaders—Asaph, Jeduthun, and Heman—directly reported to King David, serving as both spiritual and musical guides (1 Chronicles 25:6–7). A crucial element we can observe here is the musicians' training and direction under their leaders, coupled with their submission to spiritual authority.

For pastors, ministers, or leaders, this historical example is instructive. Even one good, worshiping musician/singer who carries the spirit of revival worship, and you are ready to set in motion this kind of Spirit-led worship in your ministry. This book is designed to assist in training your revival worship influencers. While I must conclude this chapter, it's crucial to emphasize that as their pastor, you should be the first to embrace the essence of prophetic worship. This book is also intended for your benefit.

Chapter 7

Revival Worshipers Filled with the Holy Spirit

Revival worship goes beyond singing a song that moves our emotions. It involves living a lifestyle of intimacy with the Holy Spirit. When you lead a song, it will be palpable that you are an intimate worshiper of God, a living sacrifice before the Lord.

When you worship from the intimate place, it releases the tones of the throne of the Father to earth. Revival will not come through us because we have a pretty voice or are super talented. It's not about us; it is about *Him*.

Why are we more worried about having the best musicians than the most intimate worshipers? Intimate worshipers are made in the furnace of the secret place, not in practice rooms or rehearsals. Although I consider that to be also important, it is not the most essential criterion when we want to become revival worshipers and conduits for the river of God.

Revival is a new swift move of God that will only come for the hungry and only through *humble* worshipers who have only one agenda—the Father's agenda!

Jesus said that His worshipers do not live by bread alone

but by every word that comes from the mouth of God (see Matthew 4:4).

Jesus also says that God blesses those who hunger and thirst for righteousness because they will be satisfied (see Matthew 5:6).

David,, the psalmist, was a man after God's heart, longing for God as the deer longs for streams of water (see Psalm 42:1).

It is crucial as revival worshipers that we hunger for more of God and be filled continually with the Holy Spirit. He is our main and most powerful fountain and source for everything. Life has its challenges, and we will always have to face them. If we are not watchful, these challenges can weigh our hearts down, dull our worship, or, even worse, shut down our spirit of worship. This has happened to me in the past.

Jesus warned us against this, saying, "Watch out! Don't let your hearts be dulled by carousing and drunkenness, and by the worries of this life. Don't let that day catch you unaware" (Luke 21:34).

There are two things mentioned in this scripture that dull our hearts: Drunkenness and the worries of this life. When you look at what the word "dull" means, it's talking about being intoxicated, not sharp, blunt, being like a dull knife, causing boredom, uninteresting, tedious, not lively or spirited, not bright, dim, slow in motion or action, mentally slow, lacking brightness of mind, and somewhat stupid.[1]

When the worries of this life become so strong in our hearts, it also robs us of our joy. And you remember that the word of God says that the joy of the Lord is our strength (see Nehemiah 8:10). This is why Jesus says to watch out! Don't let your heart be filled with these worries of life, which could make you unproductive and ruin your life. Instead, we must be filled by the Holy Spirit. But how is this possible? How can we be filled with the Holy Spirit?

The word of God tells us how in the following scripture:

Don't be drunk with wine because that will ruin your life. Instead, be filled with the Holy Spirit, singing psalms and hymns and spiritual songs among yourselves, and making music to the Lord in your hearts. And give thanks for everything to God the Father in the name of our Lord Jesus Christ. (Ephesians 5:18–20)

How do we get filled with the Holy Spirit? I believe we make it more complicated than it is. Nonetheless, this scripture guides us to be continually filled with the Holy Spirit. I find it intriguing and insightful that the word of God puts it so simply.

SINGING PSALMS AND HYMNS

We usually think that if we are not natural singers, we leave it up to the singers, but we all must sing to the Lord even if we are not professional singers. We might not be able to sing on a microphone as worship leaders, but we must all sing.

Sing to God. Believe it or not, singing psalms and hymns takes faith and emotional and mental energy. It takes an intentional effort to stop thinking of the worries of life and start singing to God and declaring His mighty works. Regardless of how we feel at any given time, God should be our priority. When you don't feel like worshiping, you must because God deserves our undivided honor and worship regardless of our feelings. Feelings can take us on a long trip to places we never intended to be. We will either live by faith or by feelings. As revival worshipers, we must learn to live by faith.

As a composer, every song I have written comes with a story, a testimony, an experience, or a new revelation. When I started writing my own songs, I was doing it without revelation, and I would just pick whatever words and sounds I could invent or find. But the words were not filled with the flow of the

Spirit because I still lacked that deep revelation of worship. When I choose a song by another composer to sing, I must first comprehend and experience it. If I don't get that experience or revelation, I don't like to use it in my worship.

What is the story you are singing about today?

Practice singing the psalms, hymns, and spiritual songs with thankful hearts. Singing the word of God is one of the best ways to go deeper into scripture and dwell in all its richness (see Colossians 3:16).

SINGING SPIRITUAL SONGS AMONGST YOURSELVES

When we sing spiritual songs, we are not singing as usual. It is singing the song of the Lord. It is singing from the tones on the throne. You are singing the Father's songs, releasing the breath of God, and creating an atmosphere filled with the Spirit and His word.

This is a heavenly atmosphere. It could be singing in tongues, a prophecy, or a declaration into the spiritual realm. This is my favorite way of singing. It is the most powerful way to sing. Miracles happen during these times of singing spiritual songs. Heavens open, and there is a release of the revelation of His word and power.

Worship, especially prophetic worship, can be a life-changing experience. It was for me.

MAKING MUSIC TO THE LORD IN YOUR HEARTS

I wonder how many songs I have missed because I let my heart become dulled by the worries of this life. When our hearts are dimmed by drunkenness and the anxieties of this life, we cannot make music to the Lord. All we can think of are our problems and difficulties, and we start complaining or murmuring instead of worshiping God with thanksgiving.

I find it intriguing that drunkenness is put next to the worries of life. Many people drink because their hearts have become overwhelmed with worries; they want to forget their problems and have a happy hour or night. They want to mentally bail out their problems by intoxicating their hearts with wine. But the word of God says to be filled with the Holy Spirit instead.

On the other hand, when we make music to the Lord, joyful and sweet creative sounds continuously flow from our lips, filling our hearts with His Spirit. Through worship, we open our hearts to Him, even if it's just a humming sound like a bird. I notice that when I sing throughout the day, I feel this mellowing joy and peace that comes over my life. I find myself saying things like, "Thank You, Lord! I love You, Father! Lord, You are so beautiful! You are mighty and powerful!" It's a continuously flowing stream of sounds and tones of the throne in my heart.

Then when it's time to worship publicly, the sounds of heaven and the tones of the throne start to flow easily because I live there daily. The devil will war against this flow, trying to fill us with the worries of life so that he can dull our hearts out of that flow of the Spirit. It has happened to me many times.

This is a ferocious war. It takes you sticking to your guns and overcoming the worries of life every day. How do we do this? Keep a prayer life and continually get to know God in a deeper way through His word and the 1200-plus names and attributes of God in the second part of this book. As we get to know God more, we get to overcome.

. . .

GIVING THANKS FOR EVERYTHING TO THE FATHER IN JESUS' NAME

When we thank the Lord, we acknowledge that all is good because He is in control. God is still sitting on His throne; therefore, if my life belongs to Him and I have given Him control over my future, then the best thing to do is to thank Him for everything, even during our apparent difficulties and disappointments.

This is where I say if we want to be useful to God as worshipers who bring revival, we must be thankful to God at all times. I know sometimes our emotions want to control us, but we must learn to surrender even our own emotions. Our emotions cannot be our God. Take up your cross, deny yourself, and follow Christ. Be willing to suffer and even die for His name's sake. This is expensive—but *true*—worship.

When we are submerged in Him through worship and prayer, the enemy's attacks will not be felt the same way. When we live in this kind of intimate relationship with God our Creator, we walk in the shelter of the Most High. Something incredible happens when we are dressed with God's glorious presence that protects us from the enemy. The battles are not felt the same way. It is as if you are just going along for a ride.

I've read the following scripture since I was eight but never had the deeper revelation until recent years. This is the incredible thing that happens when we are true worshipers filled with His Holy Spirit and powerful presence; rephrased into my own words:

You find rest in the shadow of the Almighty. He becomes your refuge and place of safety; he rescues you from every trap and protects you from deadly diseases. He covers you with his feathers and shelters you with his wings. His faithful promises become your armor and protection. Fear flees away from you. Even if a thousand fall at your side or ten thousand might die around you, these evils will not touch you. All you have to do is open your eyes and see how the wicked are punished. And because you have made the Lord your refuge and the Most High your shelter through your worship lifestyle, no evil will conquer you; no plague will come near your home. He will order his angels to protect you wherever you go, and they will hold you up with their hands, so you won't even hurt your foot on a stone. You will trample upon spiritual lions and cobras and spiritually crush the fierce lions and serpents under your feet! You are his valuable treasure. The Lord will rescue you because you love Him. He will protect you because you trust in His name. When you call on Him, He will answer you. He will be with you in trouble and will rescue and honor you. Finally, He will reward you with a long life and give you His salvation. (Psalm 91:1–16)

These are all amazing promises of God over those who love Him, focus on Him, and worship Him wholeheartedly. When worshipers are filled with the Holy Spirit, we have the Spirit of prophecy in us, and we can prophesy as we sing, dance, or play an instrument. We are also continually filled with unspeakable joy and peace. And, since we are filled with the Holy Spirit, He fills us with His spiritual gifts and His fruit (see Luke 1:67–68, Acts 13:52). So, when I worship God, I am totally equipped by Him to function and flow in the prophetic and grow in the fruit of the Spirit.

Get to know the Holy Spirit of God and fill yourself with His presence every day. He is Your protection; He is your all, the One you really need. Every worshiper must have this personal altar time with God. The Bible talks about this in both the New and Old Testaments.

THE FIRE MUST NOT GO OUT

Scriptures command that the fire of our altars must be kept burning, so it never goes out. Each morning, just like the priests in the Old Testament practiced, we need to add fresh wood to the fire and arrange the burnt offering of our lives as a sacrifice of worship to God. This could mean our calendars, agendas, time, jobs, positions, money, and especially our will and heart (see Leviticus 6:12–13).

We must attend to and maintain the fire of God on our personal altars. This is a matter of life or death. We cannot live a life independent from God. We were not made to live without God. Therefore, we could not function successfully without God, at least not in a long term. We must continually encounter Him in the secret place, His altar. We need His holy fire burning in our hearts continuously and passionately. *This fire must burn in our hearts continually at all times. It must never go out.*

Our personal altar with God is a place of purification, and we must attend to the fire of His holiness in our lives every day. Without holiness, no one will ever see the Lord. Without holiness, we cannot enter into an intimate relationship with God or know Him intimately. The fire of His holiness within us is a profound responsibility, akin to a sacred flame that requires constant tending. This spark from God, fueling our worship and guiding our spiritual journey, demands our vigilant care.

Have you witnessed the aftermath of a fire left unattended? Its destructive power is immense. In the same way, this anointed flame that illuminates our path and empowers our faith can become a destructive force if neglected. To nurture this holy fire, we must engage regularly in prayer and worship, keeping our connection with God strong and our hearts aligned with His purpose. The holy fire of God is not merely a gift; it is a sacred responsibility. This fire illuminates our path and, if not revered, has the power to consume us.

Take time today to attend to the fire of His holiness in your life if you still have not. This will burn all impurities and purify you. And, when you minister worship to God, you will not be guilty of making strange and unauthorized fire as Nadab and Abihu, the sons of Aaron did, and died as a consequence.

Get the firewood and oil of the Spirit in your life today. You will be able to confront this day prepared with the fire of God. You will be operating with the Spirit of fire and holiness. It will be a happy day filled with revelation. Seek the fire of His holiness today with all your heart! Make yourself a medallion of gold in your heart with the words, "Holy is the Lord" (see Exodus 39:30–31) Walk in holiness before Him.

Remember how John 6:62–64 says that the very words He has spoken to you are spirit and life. To be a revival worshiper that carries the breath (*pneuma*) of the Spirit of Life, you must continually seek to be filled and aligned with the Holy Spirit of God every day. Our worship must be more than music; it must be joined with the Spirit who gives life. It is His Spirit who empowers us to fulfill His purposes. His words are filled with the spirit (*pneuma*, or God's breath) and life! Align your words today to His words and sing His breath throughout this day over your daily life and challenges. Then watch how the Spirit gives life to your heart and empowers you to overcome and conquer.

As I write these words with tears in my eyes and a hungry heart, I pray and cry out: Oh Lord, resurrect our spirit of worship through Your life-giving Spirit! Forgive our sins, purify our hearts, and fill and overwhelm us with Your intimate Holy Spirit's fire and love.

Chapter 8

What Makes Worship Key to Revival?

Worship is eternal, and it will never pass because God will never stop being the Almighty God, and worshipers will never stop worshiping Him, including the angels. True worship aligns us with His word and His will. Worship refocuses our hearts onto who He is and who we are to Him.

Now, worship is more than just music. It has more to do with the condition of the heart and mind. Songs have a spirit and attitude behind them. Songs are words that have a message. Jesus said that *the words you speak* come from *the heart,* which can defile a person (see Matthew 15:16–20).

This is why God commands us to guard our hearts above all else, for it determines the course of our lives (see Proverbs 4:23). When we worship Him in spirit and truth, we are choosing the words that align us with who He is, and it inevitably puts our focus on Him. This pleases the Lord. His eyes search the whole earth for this kind of worshiper whose hearts are fully committed to Him (see 2 Chronicles 16:9).

Worship is a matter of the heart. If our hearts are fully

committed to Him, we are strengthened by Him, not by applause or pats on the back. We are ignited by His loving presence so that words start to flow from our hearts to release the life and fire of God. The word of God is spirit and life; when we align our words with His words, the atmosphere changes, and great things start to happen—first in the spiritual realm, then it manifests in the natural. God's word is the most powerful word that can exist.

Words have the power to revive or kill, so why not use them to bring revival and life to our families, cities, nation, and the world? "Death and life are in the power of the tongue, and those who love it will eat its fruit" (Proverbs 18:21 NASB).

Apart from death, if the power of life is in the tongue, can we imagine what we can do through our worship when we proclaim life over our lives, loved ones, churches, cities, and countries? We can accomplish a lot with the simplest words of praise. We can see an example of this in 2 Chronicles 20:21–22 that with just two simple praise phrases, the army of Israel won a victory without using a sword:

After consulting the people, the king appointed singers to walk ahead of the army, singing to the Lord and praising him for his holy splendor. This is what they sang: "Give thanks to the Lord; his faithful love endures forever!" At the very moment they began to sing and give praise, the Lord caused the armies of Ammon, Moab, and Mount Seir to start fighting among themselves.

They were giving thanks to the Lord while facing an army of enemies that far outnumbered them. Oh, but the next phrase was comforting: His faithful *love* endures forever. God's steadfast love was with them, just as Psalm 91 promises—He was their protection and vindicator. But first, *give thanks to the Lord*!

Honestly, this must have taken a lot of faith and committed

love. This is exactly what happens when we worship God in spirit and truth; our faith is catapulted to higher levels where we feel secure and hidden in Him from our enemy. This is why the enemy cannot find us when we are so intertwined in God's presence; he is blinded by the glorious shine of God's presence.

Worship takes our focus off us and refocuses us on Him, the Almighty I Am. True worship and praise bind the enemy's forces. This type of worship hides us in the highest hiding place with Christ, so when we worship, we fight the worst battles the easiest way because God fights our battles for us when He sees us delighting in Him. This is not related to musical instruments or voices; it is all about our hearts. He desires this and finds joy in us. We should delight lavishly in Him as well.

The enemy loses ground wherever there is worship in spirit and truth. God inhabits the praises of His people. As we are seated with Him in the heavenly realms united with Christ, we worship Him, facilitating an atmosphere where God can be enthroned and where His glory can permeate the atmosphere of our cities (see Ephesians 2:6). This, in turn, causes a spiritual revolution of the miraculous and supernatural. It helps us conquer territories and releases a spirit of holiness over the land where we worship. This level of worship is key to bringing revival.

Are you ready to be a channel and a conduit of revival? If you are reading this book, then you are!

Chapter 9

Who is The Worship For?

I hear of worship wars in churches, a war of music styles, and generational style preferences. Isn't worship supposed to be for God rather than for us or our preferences?

If worship styles are designed to please humans, then they are not true worship but entertainment. Consider the incident of the golden calf, when the Israelites, unwilling to wait for God, pressured Aaron to create a golden calf for worship. Aaron knew it was wrong, yet he yielded to the people's desires, which amounted to blasphemy. Whenever we seek to please people in worship, we risk veering into pagan practices. It could even become 'strange-fire' worship. We must keep our worship free of politics and the contamination of ego and pride. Worship is not for us; it is for Him.

This leads me to address another crucial truth regarding biases in the kingdom of God. I often hear the younger generation mocking and rejecting older people, saying, 'We are the ones bringing revival.' Similarly, I hear others claim that revival will come through them because they are "better candidates" for it. I used to be one of them. I once believed this, but over the years, God has revealed several truths to me. I have come to understand that God does not show favoritism based on age or race, as He is no respecter of persons (see Romans 2:11).

Revival is not confined to any one age group or race. It is for the humble, those who love and seek God, and those hungry to delve deeper into His Nature and Character. *Revival does not discriminate!* It embraces the young and old, the poor and rich, the educated and uneducated. The only essential elements are a *childlike faith* and a humble longing for His Presence (see Matthew 18:3–4, 5:3-6; Psalm 42:2; Isaiah 55:1; John 7:37).

God gives strength to the weary and power to the weak. The Bible says that even the young will grow weary and fall exhausted, but those who wait on the Lord will renew their strength. They will soar on wings like eagles; they will run and not grow weary; they will walk and not be faint (Isaiah 40:29–31).

We all inhabit the same era as long as we are alive at the same time. I firmly believe that every age and cultural group has unique strengths and weaknesses, contributing to the diversity that strengthens the body of Christ. Each individual offers distinct functions and callings. We need each other and should honor one another, recognizing we are living together in this generation for such a time as this. However, it is vital to remember that the Bible does not suggest that God favors anyone based on age, wealth, education, talent, race, or culture. Such a belief, which elevates one's status above fellow believers, is fundamentally ignorant, self-centered, and contrary to biblical teachings.

God consistently operates outside the confines of human perspectives and expectations. One thing I have come to understand about God is that His ways transcend human reasoning and logic. He deliberately selects what the world deems as foolish to confound those who believe themselves to be wise, strong, or highly qualified. He also favors the seemingly powerless to confound those who hold positions of power, regardless of age, wisdom, strength, or intellect. God utilizes what the world dismisses as worthless, insignificant, or inconsequential to dismantle the structures that the world esteems. Deliberately, God chooses the 'nobodies' to expose the superficial claims of the 'somebodies.' In doing so, God prevents us from ever boasting in His presence (see to 1 Corinthians 1:27–31).

Revival comes through any human who has a childlike faith, spends time intentionally at God's feet seeking His countenance in humility and holiness, worships Him in spirit and truth, and is hungry for more of His presence and His word. He looks for those who depend on Him for strength and power. Worship starts with a sincere heart of gratitude; yet *prophetic revival worship* arises from our intimacy with God.

What I like about prophetic worship is that sometimes there is no style, no specific rhythm, or time constraints. Sometimes there are not even words, just the fragrance of His presence. Yes, I know this makes some of my brethren uncomfortable, but isn't worship supposed to be for God and about God? Why are we even considering our comfort?

We are to delight and satisfy Him and *only* Him. It's all about Him. Always! It is never about us or our talents. Sometimes people like the pulpit ministry of worship because of popularity and self-glory—maybe sometimes unwittingly—but this is a wrong approach to something so sacred as the worship to our God. This is common in the secular world, but since it is not about us, we should not be obsessed with our talents. We must be careful not to worship our talents or the songs. We must humbly keep our hearts free of ourselves and full of His Spirit. I recognize this could often happen due to a lack of revelation of true worship or Inadequate training on the subject, but I hope this book will train you and others regarding true revival worship.

Even though worship to God must be done with excellence to the best of our abilities, it's not about who sings better, plays better, or has more instruments or musicians (or the best pads or who made it to the 'top'). Worship is never about you or me, so we do not take worship for ourselves.

It is about uniting all the worshipers on earth, like the angels, 24 elders, and four living creatures around God's throne in heaven, all with their unique personalities. We work to bring the whole world to its knees in worship of the Almighty I Am of the universe. Our goal is to facilitate a new revelation of God's glorious Nature and character for the people we lead in worship. As they get this revelation they can find their identity through Christ. Everyone needs to be on this journey.

We must ensure that our motivation in worship ministry is to honor God, the Author and King of all creation with no end to His names, and to acknowledge His sovereignty over all, even our worship style or songs.

Worship in heaven is a combination of sounds, powerful declarations, decrees, words, and utterances of God, about God, and to God. Since worship is always about God and not us, our sounds must be fully aligned and intertwined with the Father's songs from heaven. This is what is happening with those who are victorious over the beast, his image, and the number of His name in the book of Revelation. They were holding harps of God. They sang the song of Moses and the song of the Lamb. These are the powerful declarations of worship they made:

"Great and marvelous are Your works, O Lord God, the Almighty; righteous and true are Your ways, King of the nations! Who will not fear, O Lord, and glorify Your name? For You alone are holy; For all the nations will come and worship before

You, For Your righteous acts have been revealed." (Revelation 15:3–4 NASB)

In Revelation 14, we find another important event. The saints who kept themselves pure as virgins, following the Lamb wherever He goes, sang a new song that was so organic and so new that no one else could sing it. Not the angels, not the 24 elders, not even the four living beings could sing that song. Only the redeemed from the earth could sing this wonderful new song,

"This great choir sang a wonderful new song in front of the throne of God and before the four living beings and the twenty-four elders. No one could learn this song except the 144,000 who had been redeemed from the earth" (Revelation 14:3).

There is yet another astonishing scene in this same chapter. An angel is flying through the sky, carrying the Good News to the people of every nation, tribe, and language with the following command to everyone: "*'Fear God,' he shouted. 'Give glory to him. For the time has come when he will sit as judge. Worship him who made the heavens, the earth, the sea, and all the springs of water'*" (Revelation 14:6–7).

When I read this, it makes me tremble because when God sits as a judge to judge the deeds of everyone in this world, it will be a day of wrath. Only the true worshipers will be able to stand in the fear and reverence of God to worship and give glory to the Almighty One as they have practiced on earth.

Can you picture this day? Now picture yourself there. This is going to be a big day! We must continue to practice His worship and get ready for that day. Lord, help us deepen our worship in spirit and truth—the worship You truly deserve—in honor of You and in preparation for that day soon to come!

Chapter 10

Why do We Need to Worship?

We were designed by our Creator in the most powerful worship atmosphere to worship eternally. As Isaiah 43:7 says, "'Bring all who claim me as their God, for I have made them for my glory. It was I who created them.'"

Romans 12:1–2 urges us to give our bodies to God as a living and holy sacrifice because of all He has done for us—the kind of offering He will find pleasing and acceptable as true worship. I like how *The Message* practically puts It, "Take your everyday, ordinary life—your sleeping, eating, going-to-work, and walking-around life—and place it before God as an offering."

Worship is the key to His presence. We cannot go before God with empty words; we must have praise and worship on our lips and hearts if we want access to His inner courts. He is a mighty king, and no one comes before Him without worship. Even preaching of the word will end one day, but worship and praise to God will never end because it is heaven's grandiloquence and sophisticated way of life. We must honor God at all times to walk in intimacy with Him. Honor is big for our Father in Heaven.

If we don't honor Him in worship, we die. God does not need our worship; we need it. We need to worship because we were created during myriads and myriads of worshiping angels in the midst of God's mighty presence. We came originally from a heavenly worshiping atmosphere, so we must worship our Creator. Our Lord knew you before He formed you in your mother's womb. Before you were born, He set you apart and appointed you as His prophetic worshiper to the nations (see Jeremiah 1:5).

When we worship God, we recognize His value to us. We are refocusing our minds and synchronizing our spirit with His Spirit; we are aligning with heaven's atmosphere. We acknowledge Him as our Creator, origin, and *all*-powerful God. We dethrone ourselves and enthrone Him in our hearts and minds. As we praise His name, we also acknowledge and recognize all He has done, does, or will do for us in the past, present, and future. Our spirit and soul recognize this! That is why we must thank God, for we were fearfully and wonderfully made and because His works are wonderful, and our soul knows it very well (see Psalm 139:14).

I love what Les Brown says, "We are a masterpiece because we are a piece of the Master." I would go even further and say you are a masterpiece because you are a treasured, planned piece that the Great Master of the universe designed! Just as Ephesians 2:10 says, "For we are God's masterpiece. He has created us anew in Christ Jesus, so we can do the good things he planned for us long ago."

God created us amid the beauty and splendor of His majesty, in the midst of angels numbering myriads of myriads and thousands of thousands, in the midst of the four living creatures and the 24 elders. We were created right in the majestic throne of the *Most High*, in the midst of the Trinity's heart—the Father, Son, and the Holy Spirit. Our origin was based on beauty, splendor, and love in the purest form ever. We were created in His majestic presence, the most intimate presence in the universe. He knew us before our parents conceived us. *He* is our true origin, not our parents.

The enemy knows this because he was created by the same Creator. He hates that we are so much more beautiful and dearly loved by our Heavenly Father. The minute we are born into this world, the enemy tries to contaminate, kill, rob, and destroy our beautiful and valuable souls. He tries to make us think that we are trash and useless. He lies to us and tries to steal our beauty by deceiving us into sin and disobedience. This ultimately, if allowed, will indeed destroy our beauty and happiness. But the devil is a liar and should not be allowed to rob us of living beautiful lives with the Originator of our lives, our King and Lord.

If our origin is beautiful, our future is also beautiful and splendid. The enemy tried to take away from us the blessing of a deep, intimate relationship with our originator and our original beauty and freedom. But Jesus came and took it back from him and then gave it back to us. We are now back to the original. But it's your decision to believe it and take possession of this blessing.

After understanding this essential truth about myself, I can now enjoy a new, more intimate, and enhanced relationship with my Creator. I know I've felt ugly inside many times during my journey with the Lord, but after this revelation, I now feel so special and beautiful because I came from beauty and was created in the midst of divine beauty and splendor. Since we were created by divine, majestic hands full of love and tenderness, then our origin is based on His divine, great love, and our life will feel at home when we practice receiving and giving that type of love from which we originated and to which we will return one day. God is love. We come from it. If we could understand this, we would not have self-esteem deficiencies. Instead, we can enjoy life beautifully because our origin says so. How awesome is our Creator! This is why we must worship Him forever!

We need to worship because it's a way to show God that we recognize His sovereignty and eternal government over the human race. We must worship because it reminds us that we are nothing without Him and depend totally on Him (see John 15:5). We must worship because worship is the language of heaven and connects us with our Father's heart.

Truthfully, everyone worships something or someone. This is why Exodus 20:3–4 says that we should not have other gods or make for ourselves a carved image or any likeness of anything in heaven above, on the earth beneath, or in the water below. God is the only one that should be worshiped. How can a cat worship another cat? Or how can a horse worship another horse? In other words, how can humans idolize or worship other humans when they are equally created and made of the same materials? Or how can human beings worship objects which are extremely inferior to them? We are to worship the only One Who is above all creation—The Father. We owe our life to Him. He is our source of life and eternal salvation, and happiness.

This is why "I will sing to the Lord as long as I live. [And] I will praise my God to my last breath!" I want "all my thoughts be pleasing to him, for I rejoice in the Lord" (Psalm 104:33–34).

To worship God is a commandment stated many times throughout the word. As Psalm 100 states in the first few verses: Shout, worship, come and acknowledge that the Lord is God! We are to enter His presence with thanksgiving and praise!

When we worship God in spirit and truth, we prove to the spiritual realm and the world that we honor and trust God (see Ephesians 3:10).

Chapter 11

How Should I Worship?

True worship is the mark and the seal of the redeemed through the Spirit of God! (see John 4:23-24) Worship is a trademark of the white throne in Heaven's atmosphere. There is where worship originates, but the worship of the redeemed is an exquisite, special and beautiful sound to the heavens. It's a sound that Is formed in the heart of the redeemed. Intimate worship has nothing to do with styles, rhythms, or even the talents of the musicians. It has a lot to do with how close we are to God, how much we understand about Him, and how well we understand who we are in Christ.

Worship comes from a heart of gratitude, a surrendered will, and a heart that recognizes its source of strength to live a useful, productive life through the Spirit. We acknowledge that the human spirit we carry came from the mighty throne of the Almighty I AM THAT I AM. This is His *breath,* and it belongs to Him. We carry His breath in us. When we sing in spirit and truth, we sing the breath of the Father. That breath is the same breath that He blew into our lives when we were formed and became human beings. His breath is our life. It is this breath that we must give back to God through our worship.

Worship is not limited to music; it is an expression of the heart's attitude. This expression carries its own melody, conveying the message: "I originated from You, and I will ultimately return to You. My eternal allegiance is to You; I am nothing without You, and my existence depends on You. You are my utmost priority, my dearest friend, the love of my life, and I cannot imagine living without You." These declarations are pleasing to God when they reflect the attitude of our hearts.

When I worship God, I surrender my will, heart, talents, and whole being unto Him. Surrendering is a major part of how we should worship, letting go of our human logic and letting the Spirit flow through our worshiping hearts.

I don't enjoy performing because it diverts my attention away from Him. This is why I keep my worship as simple as possible, not too busy, or eloquent. I just be myself. I don't attempt to mimic other musicians or singers. I believe that one of the most astonishing things God did in creation is that He created everyone with their own uniqueness. Many musicians or singers like to copy those they consider better than themselves, but God wants your worship to be skillfully and organically original. He made you to be an original, not a copy of an original.

Also, to have acceptable worship before Him, our mouths must be holy and pure from murmuring and complaining. I cover this subject best in my book, The Killer of Revival: Murmuring, but I'll tell you that if you want to keep a connection with heaven through your worship, you must not let your mouth be contaminated with any foul language, murmuring, complaining, or negativity, which comes from lack of faith and ungratefulness. Your mouth must be a praising mouth and a pure spring of water. James teaches us about the power and responsibility of our words. It emphasizes that we should use our tongues to give thanks to our Lord and Father and not to curse others who are also created in the likeness of God. This passage reminds us that words of thanksgiving and cursing should not come from the same mouth, just as a spring of water cannot pour out both sweet and bitter water from the same source. (see James 3:9–11)

I have a saying that goes like this: "When you complain, blessings run away. When you praise, blessings come your way. So, let's sing in praise, 'til our hearts brightly blaze, with all His blessings, our souls will be amazed. Yet true godliness, with contentment as our wealth, is the greatest treasure, a store of spiritual health." (see 1 Timothy 6:6)

As true worshippers, it's crucial to avoid murmuring and grumbling in our daily lives. Although there may be moments when we are tempted to complain, we must combat this by immersing ourselves in the word of God. Renewing our minds continually with God's word is essential, and we should make a conscious effort to do so. By doing this, we can find continuous reasons to worship God in spirit and truth, knowing that it all begins in our minds, hearts, and mouths.

Therefore, let's give our bodies to God because of all He has done for us. Let us be a living and holy sacrifice that He will find acceptable. We must understand that this is truly the way to worship Him. Let's not copy the behavior and customs of the world in which we live, but instead, let God transform us into a new person by changing the way we think. This is how we will learn to know God's will for our lives, which is good, pleasing, and perfect (see Romans 12:1–2).

Let's take David's example in Psalm 56; when the Philistines seized him in Gath while he was in the middle of turmoil, he decided to pray, praise, worship, and trust in God and His promises. He sang to the Lord, remembering these truths he later wrote in Psalm 136, strengthening him to worship in spirit and truth:

Give thanks to the Lord, for he is good! His faithful love endures forever. Give thanks to the God of gods. His faithful love endures forever. Give thanks to the Lord of lords. His faithful love endures forever. Give thanks to him who alone does mighty miracles. His faithful love endures forever. (Psalm 136:1–4)

Chapter 12

How to Develop a Worshiping Heart

A heart inclined toward worship develops through gratitude and thanksgiving. The Bible encourages this approach in Psalm 100:4: "Enter his gates with thanksgiving; go into his courts with praise. Give thanks to him and praise his name."

To cultivate such a heart, begin by honoring God with your gratitude, which glorifies His name. Psalm 29:1–2 emphasizes this, stating, "Honor the LORD, you heavenly beings; honor the LORD for his glory and strength. Honor the LORD for the glory of his name. Worship the LORD in the splendor of his holiness."

Express gratitude in all circumstances, even during challenging times. Practicing thankfulness aligns with God's will and pleases Him. If you are new to this practice, it may initially seem difficult, but as you deepen your understanding of who is Jesus Christ, your sense of gratitude will naturally grow.

The Apostle Paul serves us as an example of this practice. Despite his trials and imperfections, he consistently expressed gratitude for everything and everyone. He continually would express phrases like in 1 Corinthians 1:4, "I always thank my God for you," and in Ephesians 1:16, "I have not stopped thanking God for you.

This was a phrase Paul used numerous times in his letters to the brethren in different cities. We can ask ourselves, why did Paul constantly repeat this phrase? Why did he always thank God for this and that?

This scripture revealed to us why: “Be thankful in all circumstances, for this is God’s will for you who belong to Christ Jesus. Do not stifle [quench] the Holy Spirit” (1 Thessalonians 5:18–19). Paul wanted to do God’s will and didn’t want to quench, stifle, or sadden the Holy Spirit of God in his life.

Even as I write this, I had to pause to raise my hands to the sky and ask God for forgiveness for all the times that, in the midst of my trials, I forgot to give thanks because I was more focused on my circumstances. God has taught me that being grateful is essential for living a successful life in this journey we call life. This pleases him very much.

If we desire to do God’s will in our lives but are unsure of how to, here is the answer: Be thankful in all circumstances. This is the will of God for our lives in Christ. Why is it so important to be thankful in all circumstances? Because otherwise, we would stifle, quench, sadden, and put out the Spirit’s fire in our life. Wouldn’t your joy be quenched, or at least saddened, if your son or daughter were ungrateful to you after you made a big sacrifice for him or her? The Holy Spirit will even be more saddened when we are ungrateful to God and won’t give Him thanks for everything and everyone!

He desires us to have a grateful heart because this helps us become real worshipers in spirit and truth. Practice giving thanks to God for everything and everyone throughout the day.

Avoid complaining, murmuring, negativity, and everything that does not seem to come from a grateful heart. When a challenge comes, first give thanks to God in prayer and ask for His direction in that situation, then wait (see Psalm 42:5).

Pray and wait; he won't be late. God will give you the answer. He is never late, and He never loses a battle. This should be an attitude of the heart practiced every day of the year. Remember that God fills all things everywhere with Himself, and nothing is out of His reach. Your thanksgiving will position you for blessing in your life always. Determine to give thanks to God in everything and for everyone in prayer from this day on. Have a day filled with thanksgiving and blessing!

Get to know God for who He is. Start by intentionally consecrating a corner in your home, separated just for you to encounter God and His word every day. Every worshiper must have this sacred space. It is where all life comes from, the fountain and source of our worship. I call it the Holy Spirit room/corner, my weeping place. Moses called it the tent of meeting (see Exodus 33:7). Make an appointment to meet Him there every day. Go in there with no rush. Learn to wait in His presence. There will be times when all you'll do is weep in His presence. Every time I weep with an open heart before God, He always answers me!

The Psalmist knew the secret of spending time in "this beautiful place of worship [that] beats thousands spent on Greek island beaches" (Psalm 84:10–11 MSG). By intentionally being in that place of worship, you keep the fire burning and add wood to the fire. God made us to be dependent on Him for everything. If you keep the fire burning in your relationship with God, you will become an intimate worshiper whom He can trust to bring His revival fire to others. As it says in the scriptures, "Remember, the fire must be kept burning on the altar at all times. It must never go out" (Leviticus 6:13).

Know all the names and attributes of God and study each of them separately. Make sure you read through to the very end of this book, so you see God's twelve hundred-plus names and attributes. If you meditate on at least three a day, you will be munching on one hundred names and attributes of God per month, and this will add up to twelve hundred a year. Can you imagine what will happen in a year? Did you know that the enemy does not want you to know this? This is why I went through a ferocious war to write this book.

Ask God to reveal Himself to you. When you realize what a powerful God you serve, you will be amazed at what this will do for your life. Get to know your purpose in life. Why did God create you and who you are to Him? If you can find your purpose on this earth assigned by the Creator, your soul will be so grateful and joyous, and you will live a very exciting life.

In order to develop a heart of worship, it is crucial to learn to forgive and live free from hatred or resentment. If you need help with this, start by asking the Holy Spirit for assistance. He is both able and willing to guide you through this process. You don't even need to make an appointment; He is always available. If you don't how to do this, consider reaching out to a spiritually mature leader who can pray for and guide you through this journey. Above all, remember when you love God, you will want to obey Him and submit your emotions and mind completely to Him. When you obey God by forgiving others, then the Father will forgive your sins. This forgiveness sets you free through the power of Jesus Christ. It is ultimately and primarily your decision to break free. God has empowered you to overcome through Christ! However, you bear the responsibility for the emotions you allow to linger in your life. Once you decide to do your part as a human, God will fulfill His role by healing and helping you overcome. Remember, for those who love God, everything works for their best (see Romans 8:28).

To develop a worshiping heart, you also need to keep your eyes pure and holy. You become what you feed through your eyes and ears. Watch your mind, your spirit, and your mouth. Don't let anyone poison your spirit, no matter who it is. Just as you wouldn't allow anyone to dump a can of garbage in the middle of your bedroom, the same principle applies to your spirit. Keep your heart pure and clean. Keep your mind filled with the word of God, His Names and His promises. Keep a song or a tune in your heart all day long, like a constant drip of water, to maintain that flow of worship throughout the day and night.

Learn to be humble and submissive to your authorities. This is a great sign of a healthy and mature heart. If you can't submit to authority, you won't be able to live and minister with authority. Your worship will lack authority. God will not grant you authority until you learn to submit to His established earthly authorities. I recognize that this view is not popular in America, but it is the principle of God, not mine (see Hebrews 13:17, 1 Peter 2:13-17, Romans 13:1-2).

Ask God to show you how to worship Him better and to make you a true worshiper who worships in spirit and truth.

Finally, never give up! Keep pressing in. God desires this even more than you do, and He will soon pour out His glorious Presence. Never cease your worship; your very life depends on it, for this is your primary calling and your destiny.

As we all go to our homes or places of worship, keep in mind the password to His Presence. Thanksgiving from the heart as it is described in the Message in Psalm 100:4–5, "Enter with the *password*: 'Thank you' Make yourselves at home, talking praise. Thank him. Worship him. For God is sheer beauty, all-generous in love, loyal always and ever." (emphasis added)

Let's start using this password at least seven times a day and enter His presence, thanking Him for His love, mercy and faithfulness. Start developing a worshiping heart today!

Chapter 13

What Happens When We Worship God In Spirit & Truth?

It takes faith to worship God in spirit and truth. It takes love to worship with faith, it takes revelation to worship with love, and the result is intimacy with God. Something supernatural happens when a redeemed-by-the-blood soul worships in spirit and truth. It is the highest level of spirituality. The way we worship God reveals a lot about where our hearts are with God. It shows the level of relationship we have with Him. It is hard to worship God if you don't know Him, trust Him, or truly believe in Him. Conversely, your worship deepens as you get to know God better and discover who you truly are to Him. Also, it is good to know that your worship to God does grow in levels.

You first start with blind first love. From there, it grows into worship with revelation and understanding. Then the spirit of worship takes ahold of you taking you into higher levels of God's glory where everything is possible and perfect in Him. When you touch His perfection, you are radically changed into a different person. Words have power, therefore, because we are pronouncing words in our worship. We can release life, the very life of the Spirit (see Prov. 18:21).

The process of taking your worship to God on a deeper level will be challenged and attacked by the enemy. The enemy's goal is to shut down your worship because he loses ground every time you get deeper into the spirit of worship. It's all about returning to our origin; the enemy doesn't want us to discover our place of origin and the plans of our Creator for our lives. One reason is that when we worship in spirit and truth, there are breakthroughs, the enemy's works are destroyed, and the kingdom of God comes and takes over that territory. Darkness loses ground, and more worshipers join the army of worshipers. The Father is looking for true worshipers who will bring His glory to the earth to see a worldwide revival of salvation, healing, deliverance, and prosperity.

Please do not think for a minute that I am talking about just music or singers. I'm referring to the kind of worship that comes from a grateful and surrendered heart. This is a lifestyle, but not a stagnant one. It is a growing, flowing, and increasing desire to be close to God, do His will, live for Him, please Him, and delighting in Him by finding pleasure in Him regularly. It is like drinking the best and highest quality wine and getting under the influence of His mighty and glorious Presence. It is returning to our origin and desiring to stay there eternally. It is an ardent desire for our Bridegroom, as we will soon be married in the Lamb's divine wedding, the day we will unite for eternity.

Ah, that is so romantic. I call this future event Divine Romance Day—the day of the consummation of our salvation and redemption, the day we'll be joined forever and ever to our God. How beautiful! How wonderful! How my soul awaits that day!

Many supernatural breakthroughs happen when we worship in spirit and truth. No wonder the Father is searching for such worshipers on earth. They will be the ones to bring revival to this earth. They are the channels God needs to bring His glory to earth—the revivalists, the intimates of God.

Think of what happened when the temple of Solomon was dedicated, and the Levites worshiped with their instruments. They could no longer play because the glory filled the temple!

Think about when David built a 24/7 radical and extreme tabernacle for God's Presence before the Ark of the Covenant when it was unheard of, prophetically bringing a new way and wave of intimate, spontaneous, and genuine worship a thousand years before Christ. He worshiped God with all his might and made himself undignified before all of Israel, even when his wife, Micah, ridiculed him for it. Think about all the prophetic psalms and victories that came out of these 24/7 worshipers at the tabernacle of David.

Think of King Saul's nakedness, achieved by stripping off his royal garments, which symbolized his humble submission to God, acknowledging that his kingship was subject to God's will and portraying a state of surrender and vulnerability as he was under the divine influence of God's Spirit.

Think about the 24 elders and the four living creatures, how they bow down and worship God unceasingly before the throne. Think about the tones around the throne.

Think about Paul and Silas when they were singing and worshiping instead of crying and complaining. At midnight there was a great earthquake, so the prison doors opened, and salvations followed as a result.

Think about the army of Josaphat when the singers were at the front line of the army and won a great victory by praising and delighting in God.

The Azusa Street Revival is a great example of what happens when we worship in spirit and truth. The people of God were singing spontaneous and prophetic worship at the Azusa revival, reported as a new musical phenomenon that became known as "singing in the Spirit" and noted for how it touched the world. People who attended the revival meetings cried, shouted, shrieked, sang, prophesied, fell in the Spirit, jumped, tried to carry on conversations in tongues with one another at breakneck speed, and simultaneously bore witness to what the Lord had done in their lives. It was an outpouring of God's glory that changed the world—because people gathered to worship *in spirit and truth*!

Chapter 14

Release the Atmosphere of Heaven through Your Worship

Worship leaders must lead their hearts first before leading other hearts into God's presence. This should lead us to ask, 'how do I take my worship to the next level?'

What took my worship to a new level (and continues to) was when I discovered who God truly was for me and who I was for Him. This is a lifelong journey of discovery, and it begins with just one step, but it progresses with the speed of the Spirit according to the power that works within us. (See Ephesians 3:20)

When this happens, you start singing with anointed revelation from the heavenly atmosphere. The tones of the throne begin to flow effortlessly. You will start worshiping from the fountain of truth through His Spirit. Your worship will attract the flowing river that comes from the throne of God.

This flow from the throne will start to heal both you and others. It will bring joy, peace, love, revelation, power, discernment, growth, deliverance, and salvation to all that will be touched by these living waters that flow from His throne!

It is worth it to take whatever time is necessary to get to

know who God is and who you are for Him. It's an exciting journey, though sometimes it is challenging. The good news is that you will not have to do it alone. *God wants this more than you could ever want it*! Trust me; this is not fiction; this is real! God is real! Don't be afraid to start this journey today.

We see a glimpse into the power of releasing heaven's atmosphere through worship in the story of the apostle Paul during his time in the Philippian jail (see Acts 16:11–40).

Paul stayed for several days in "Philippi, a major city of that district of Macedonia and a Roman colony" (16:12). There, he won for the Lord a businesswoman named Lydia, who was a worshiper of God. "One day, as [he] was going down to the place of prayer, [he] met a slave girl who had a spirit that enabled her to tell the future. She earned a lot of money for her masters by telling fortunes" (16:16). Paul, having discernment, cast the spirit out of this slave girl in Jesus' name, and she was instantly delivered. This infuriated her masters because Paul ruined their money-making machine. They dragged Paul and Silas to the city's authorities and falsely accused them. He and Silas were stripped and severely beaten with wooden rods and then incarcerated in the inner dungeon with their feet clamped in the stocks.

Despite this unjust, painful experience and humiliation, Paul chose to ignore the insult to his pride and instead decided to put his mind on why he was there in the first place—the sake of Christ—so he began worshiping God with Silas in the midst of it all. This is the most powerful worship that could ever be, to worship God in brokenness and pain. It's easier said than done, but nothing is impossible for those who believe as Paul and Silas did.

With his worship, Paul created an atmosphere of heaven so powerfully mighty that the glory of God came down and shook the foundations of their circumstances in both the spiritual atmosphere and the natural. Such was the power of this moment that all the prison doors were forced open because when God opens a door, no one can close it, not even with the shackles or clamps on their feet and hands as they were in that dungeon.

"Around midnight, Paul and Silas were praying and singing hymns to God, and the other prisoners were listening. Suddenly, there was a massive earthquake" because the Glory of God came in, "and the prison was shaken to its foundations. All the doors immediately flew open, and the chains of every prisoner fell off!" (16:25–26). This was such a powerful and intentional manifestation of God's glorious love that not just all the doors immediately flew open, but the chains of *every* prisoner fell off!

Ponder on this for a moment. The prisoners not only witnessed this powerful manifestation of God, but when you see that they did not try to escape, it says a lot about their experience. They had a change of heart because they tasted God's sweet, heavenly atmosphere. When the jailer realized that he did not have to take his life because all the prisoners were still there, He also received an impartation of God's glorious, loving presence. The jailer's change of heart was so profound that he became a believer and even got baptized with his family that night. He washed Paul and Silas' wounds and even fed them food in his home.

This is the kind of angelic atmosphere that always results in miracles. The divine reason Paul needed to be in prison, although unjustly, was to accomplish the jailer and his family's salvation and release God's new revelation in the prisoners' lives. The release of those prisoners and the release of the atmosphere of deliverance, salvation, and healing over that city was God's vindication against the enemy. I can't wait to meet some of those prisoners in heaven who were never the same after that powerful experience. Paul may have left that city, but the witnesses to that powerful, glorious, and eye-opening event were left to continue to testify to the power of Jesus Christ alongside the jailer and his family! The deepest love that could exist is to love in brokenness, as Jesus did. Paul followed Jesus' example.

When we worship with all our hearts amid our brokenness, we inevitably release the atmosphere of the throne—which releases miracles, healing, and salvation. But it facilitates an atmosphere of deliverance for our minds into another level of knowledge of who God is and who we are to Him. This is so critical for these last days.

Jesus told us that we would go through trials and sorrows on this earth, but He also encouraged us to take heart because He has overcome the world (see John 16:33). We, too, shall overcome as we focus on Him through our worship and praise; even as we go through war zones or are wounded and broken, we shall overcome in Jesus' mighty Name!

Chapter 15

Charge the Atmosphere with Praise and Worship

"Believe in the Lord your God,
and you will be able to stand firm."
—2 Chronicles 20:20

Jehoshaphat was very brave and had to eliminate his fears because he understood God had a perfect plan. All he needed to do was believe, obey, trust, worship, and praise to prove that he trusted God. This trust is the key ingredient in our worship, the kind of worship that wars against the enemy without fighting in the natural. Instead, Jehoshaphat knew all they were to do was worship and exalt the faithfulness of Jehovah. This released the atmosphere of victory and made them win the war without even moving a finger to fight.

By singing in worship, they were already celebrating the salvation of God even before they could humanly see it fulfilled. They filled the atmosphere with praise and worship, charging the air with the power of God and releasing the heavens, and the All-Powerful delivered them. All the enemies were destroyed, every one of them. True worship blinds and defeats the enemy!

When we charge the atmosphere with true worship, we can release the kingdom of His glory, and the result will be a new revelation of who God is and who we are to Him. We can see His power and vindication from our enemies.

When you worship in spirit and truth, you become a conduit, or channel of Heaven. The Father can trust you to release His breath and divine sound to the towns, cities, and nations. This is why the scripture says that every knee shall bow and every tongue confess that Jesus Christ is Lord (see Philippians 2:9–11, Romans 14:11). As you release His breath and the tones of the throne to earth, this will cause every knee to bow down to our God, confess Jesus Christ as Lord, and praise Him.

The greatest victories will come as you worship the Great I Am. Doors will open where it was impossible. You will prophesy the song of the Father to the people of God. God will speak to you and through you.

He will entrust new songs with His breath and divine sound to you. Some will be only for the secret place and an audience of One. Others are to be sung and heard by the nations, who will bow before the King of kings.

The glory of God will come to wherever you are worshiping. You will be a carrier of His glorious breath. You risk looking weirdly different from the other traditional singers because you will have a prophetic anointing over every territory you worship. Your worship will bring revival to your life first and then to your city, nation, and the world. This is the worship of a general in God's worship army. You need to learn this level of worship through the Spirit in the secret place. Talent or years of experience with the worship ministry will not take you there, but only the secret place. This is such a simple yet profound secret of the throne of God that many miss it.

There are two key scriptures I have always pondered in my heart. The first one talks about how we are not able to do this by our might or our power but by His Spirit (see Zechariah 4:6).

The second one is even more important to know that no matter what we can do, without Him, we can do or accomplish nothing (see John 15:5). These two scriptures are so essential in our lives as worshipers, especially when we are in the middle of a spiritual war.

We must rely totally on Him, abide in Him, and prayerfully be led by His Spirit every step of the way through our worship. We don't worship our worship; we worship the Great King of the universe. That is a huge responsibility. Start charging the atmosphere with praise and worship from the breath of the Father. The Father is looking for you.

Chapter 16

Why is The Father Seeking True Worshipers?

The Father is seeking those true worshipers whom He can trust with the Key of David. Those are the worshipers He can use to open and access the heavens and the manifestation of the presence of the Almighty, releasing them to this earth as a conduit. These worshipers cry out Jesus' words, "May Your kingdom come, and Your will be done as it is in heaven" (see Matthew 6:10).

To gain this trust, we must have a heart like the Father's. We must house in our hearts the spirit of worship, humility, and submission to God, cultivating a heart that is after God's own heart, one that does everything God tells us to do. Such the Father seeks after and to those He entrusts revival.

I have realized that worship is more powerful than many believe it to be. Singing is not the only way to worship God because worship comes from within our deepest selves. Nonetheless, I still strongly believe that as we worship God with our voices, hands, or body the way John 4:23–24 stipulates it, it connects us directly to our divine origin—*His presence.*

During these times of intensive, intimate worship, I have

received more of God, His character, His divine nature, and His power imparted straight into my spirit, soul, and body from none other than His Holy Spirit. God has spoken His secrets into my ears as I pour myself into Him without restriction or political correctness. During these times of deeply intimate worship, free of all religious forms or traditions that might hinder my full expression of worship to God, I have received a deeper understanding of His love and grace for me.

One day, my eyes were opened as I worshiped God and poured my whole self into Him in worship and honor. I saw by revelation His throne. I could not see Him, but I could see a very bright light coming from His throne. It reminded me of a picture that someone tried to paint the throne with the 24 elders and the four living creatures around the white throne. It was as if that picture had become a reality to me. All this happened as I sang a new song in the Spirit, completely surrendering myself to Him.

Then He took me back to creation when He created the first human being. He took me to Genesis 2:7, "Then the Lord God formed the man from the dust of the ground. He breathed the breath [or spirit] of life into the man's nostrils, and the man became a living person." I realized that he was just dust, like clay, and he was not a living being. But the minute that the mighty God breathed His breath into Adam's nostrils, he became a living soul.

I felt impressed by God; *where did this breath come from?* Then, He showed me the day I was created. I could see how I came to be a living soul. I came right from the gut of His mighty presence, His divine "self" through His breath! My spirit came from that mighty throne! That's when I realized that my origin was not from Puerto Rico or my parents but from His mighty presence. There, I originated as a living being, later formed in my Mother's womb. I was overwhelmed to discover that my existence originated from His mighty and splendorous throne. This was the most intimate and warm thought I'd ever had! I felt so close to Him, like never before in my life.

I got the understanding that we were created in the midst of the beauty and splendor of God's majesty. We were created in the midst of angels, numbering myriads of myriads and thousands of thousands, in the midst of the four living creatures and the 24 elders, right in the majestic throne of the *Most High*, in the midst of the Trinity's heart—the Father, Son, and the Holy Spirit. Our origin was and is based on beauty, splendor, and love in the purest form ever known. We were created in His majestic and most intimate presence in the universe. My life has never been the same after this experience. It only started a very exciting journey, and I am still walking through it.

More revelation came from this one experience as time passed. All this happened while I was singing a new song spontaneously, intimately pouring my soul into Him, abandoning, and surrendering myself to Him in the most powerful worship that could exist—in spirit and truth.

Do you want to get deeper into Him and know His secrets or mysteries? Try this type of worship, making it your lifestyle until Jesus comes.

Chapter 17

What Is True Worship?

Dr. Myles Monroe once said, "Whatever you give more worth to becomes your idol and your worth-ship." True worship comes from a heart close to God, a heart that only wants to do God's will, a heart that is according to God's heart.

It offends God when we don't honor Him with our hearts because our hearts are far from Him; as Jesus said in Matthew 15:8, "These people honor me with their lips, but their hearts are far from me."

On the other hand, as imperfect as he was, David was considered by God as a man after *His own heart*. Why? Because he did everything God wanted him to do, despite his imperfections. "But God removed Saul and replaced him with David, a man about whom God said, 'I have found David, son of Jesse, a man after my own heart. He will do everything I want him to do'" (Acts 13:22).

When you are a true worshiper after God's heart, you do everything God wants and asks you to do. Your heart is fully committed to His will.

True worship does not come from PowerPoints or hymnals.

It comes from a sincere, devoted, and hungry heart. True worship is not necessarily connected to music. It starts with a thankful heart. It is a devotion of the heart to our Creator.

True worship is a heart madly in love with God, hungry for His word and presence. It's worship from someone who allows the Holy Spirit to flow freely through him, someone who wants to make Jesus famous rather than himself or his talent, and has only one motivation and agenda in mind: to be a channel for God's glory to enter the earth.

True worship is the exuberant offering of yourself, your heart, and your mind on a platter of gold to the King of kings. It is boasting about God only, not our merits, talents, or accomplishments. "Therefore, as the scriptures say, 'If you want to boast, *boast only about the Lord*" (1 Corinthians 1:31, emphasis added).

I'm highly sensitive to those who approach worship with ego-driven intentions. I'm not suggesting that worship requires perfection, as we are all inherently imperfect worshipers due to our human nature. What I'm emphasizing is the importance of aligning your spirit and heart deeply into with who God is and who you are to Him. This alignment is what makes your heart perfect. While some may believe that flawless music is the most important element, it's crucial to understand that true worship hinges on the sincerity of our hearts, surpassing all other factors.

Something supernaturally powerful happens when we worship in spirit and truth (see John 4:23–24, Acts 16:16–34). Worshiping God in truth has to do with our hearts and sincerity. Anyone can sing, play, dance, clap their hands, or even shout, but that does not necessarily mean they worship in spirit and truth. The world does this, and they do it way more skillfully than many Christians do, but this does not mean they are worshiping God. They could worship a person, themselves, musical instruments, or an object, but not God. Worship has to come from the heart, truly from the heart. What does this mean? It means the worship that comes from our mouths must match our hearts and our sincerity—it must be truthful, intimate, and with honor to the One who created us, our source of life (see Mark 7:6).

To simplify It, our song must be filled with true love and affection for Him. If you are singing, 'I love You, I love You, I love You; You are the source of my life," is this true? Do you really love Him? Do you consider Him the source of your life when you make decisions in life?

How do you know that you truly love God? If you truly love Him, He says you will keep His commandments (live by His principles). This helps us ensure we don't sing a lie. After all, you want to sing the truth. You want to sing with understanding (see 1 Corinthians 14:15; 1 Corinthians 5:7–8; Hebrews 13:15).

Even the birds praise God every day; their praise is just a chirp (see Psalms 148:10; 150:6), but for us humans—the redeemed—we were given the Holy Spirit's power to worship God in deeper ways. There are levels of worship like what happens in Ezekiel 47 that starts with a stream flowing up to the ankles and ends with a river that is too deep to walk across. When we start praising God, it might cost us a bit if we are not already in that flowing stream of the Spirit, but as we come with a thankful heart and surrender ourselves in praise, recognizing and celebrating His mighty works, names, and attributes, this river then grows deeper and deeper. Something miraculous happens as we enter into a period of deeper worship, loving and adoring Him for who He is. The river gets deeper, and a Spirit of prophecy and revelation is released into the atmosphere, so our human agendas and programs no longer work.

At that point, we are surrounded by His glorious, loving

presence, as if He comes and kisses us back. He sets us free from burdens and restores our hearts. He reveals His intimate love to us, and He embraces us intimately.

I have seen salvations, physical healings, massive deliverances, hearts healed, and more during this highest level of intimate worship. I have also seen that this never happens in some churches because they stay with the stream at the ankles, and the deeper river won't fit their agendas or is way too uncomfortable for some people who are not used to it. It is so worth it to get to the level where you can't do anything but worship Him and stay there, surrendered, swimming, or floating on that precious river of God!

According to Psalm 15 and Psalm 101, the only people who may worship in His sanctuary, enter God's presence, stand firm forever, and serve Him, will be the ones who:

- lead blameless lives and do what is right
- speak the truth from sincere hearts
- refuse to gossip, harm their neighbors, or speak evil of their friends
- despise flagrant sinners
- honor the faithful followers of the Lord
- keep their promises even when it hurts
- cannot be bribed to lie about the innocent
- are careful to live a blameless life
- will lead a life of integrity in their own home
- will refuse to look at anything vile and vulgar
- will have nothing to do with those who deal crookedly
- will reject perverse ideas and stay away from every evil
- will not tolerate people who slander their neighbors
- will not endure conceit and pride

- will search for faithful people to be their companions
- are above reproach

God is not impressed with our religious meetings, conferences, conventions, projects, slogans, goals, egocentric music, or noisy hymns of praise. In fact, He hates it if it comes from the wrong heart. God hates hypocrisy, as He states in the following scripture:

"I can't stand your religious meetings. I'm fed up with your conferences and conventions. I want nothing to do with your religious projects, pretentious slogans, and goals. I'm sick of your fund-raising schemes, your public relations, and image-making. I've had all I can take of your noisy ego music. When was the last time you sang to *me*? Do you know what I want? I want justice—oceans of it. I want fairness—rivers of it. That's what I want. That's *all* I want." (Amos 5:21–24 MSG)

In the New Living Translation, it says:

"I hate all your show and pretense— the hypocrisy of your religious festivals and solemn assemblies. I will not accept your burnt offerings and grain offerings. I won't even notice all your choice of peace offerings. Away with your noisy hymns of praise! I will not listen to the music of your harps. Instead, I want to see a mighty flood of justice, an endless river of righteous living." (Amos 5:21–24)

You become what you celebrate, you pursue what you celebrate, you will have what you celebrate, and you are empowered by what you celebrate! What or whom are you celebrating today?

Chapter 18

Worshiping God Without Guilt

As we worship God, sometimes we can be hindered by feelings of guilt or inadequacy, but the story of the woman with the alabaster jar should inspire us greatly. When we understand this simple yet deep truth, we can overcome this hindrance and throw ourselves into Jesus' loving grace and mercy.

This woman came to Jesus while He was eating a meal, took a jar of extremely expensive perfume, and broke it, pouring the costly offering on Jesus' feet. It was such an extravagant and radical gift of worship that several religious people who saw it were offended at how lavish a gift she had given (see Luke 7:36–50). Religion always wants us to submit to what's culturally acceptable or the status quo, but a true worshiper is an all-surrendered vessel of worship to God. Radical worship takes radical surrendering.

Jesus was deeply moved by this kind of worship. The impacting words of Jesus to this woman—" Your sins are forgiven"—contain a powerful lesson. This woman was a sinner who worshiped Jesus in a costly and unusual way. This was so meaningful because it was coupled with humility and repentance. Jesus not only forgave her sins but also cleansed her from her sins. When we come with a repentant heart and a contrite spirit in worship, God will forgive our sins and purify us from wickedness because of what Jesus finished at the cross. He will not reject us. God never rejects a broken and repentant heart. He desires a broken spirit over a prideful spirit (see Psalm 51:17).

In Colossians 2:11-23, we are reminded that in Christ, we have been freed from the legalistic rituals and decrees that judge according to human standards. Christ Himself has taken our transgressions and nailed them to the cross, disarming the powers that once condemned us.

As we worship with a broken spirit before God—rejecting pride and embracing humility—He meets us with open arms of forgiveness and purification, just as He did for the woman with the alabaster jar. In worship, you will be set free from all guilt as the Sprit of grace and righteousness empowers you through Jesus Christ.

No matter how you feel, remember that the enemy is the accuser of the saints and will always try to be legalistic with you, attempting to make you feel unworthy of worshiping the Lord. When that happens, remind him that you are the righteousness of God through Jesus, and therefore you have been made right with God, for you have been set free from the power of sin and death. This is when you must worship with even greater intensity and fervor.

When we come before the Lord, we come in our weakness. As we become more aware of God's glory and glorious presence, we become more aware of our unworthiness and our absolute dependency on God for His purification and forgiveness. We can see this happen to Isaiah in the following scripture:

And I said: "Woe is me! For I am lost; for I am a man of

unclean lips, and I dwell in the midst of a people of unclean lips; for my eyes have seen the King, the Lord of hosts!" Then one of the seraphim flew to me, having in his hand a burning coal that he had taken with tongs from the altar. And he touched my mouth and said: "Behold, this has touched your lips; your guilt is taken away, and your sin atoned for." (Isaiah 6:5–7 ESV)

We continually humble ourselves before God for His mercy. We repent before Him as the Spirit convicts us. We repent of many things like: Hardened hearts, unbelief, pride, envy, jealousy, competition, seeking positions, wicked thoughts, blindness to other people's needs, selfishness, materialism, individualism, disobedience, fear of man and more.

Like the woman with the alabaster jar, we too must worship God in our brokenness, for He is good and merciful. A spirit of brokenness and worship blend beautifully together, reminding us of the potter and the clay from Jeremiah 18:6. God says, 'Like clay in the hand of the potter, so are you in my hand.' This metaphor beautifully illustrates how, in moments of worship, even when marred and broken, we remain in God's sovereign hands, perfectly positioned for reshaping.

While writing this book, I have been broken many times. However, each time I worship God amidst this brokenness, I felt my worship piercing right through the heavens, reaching the throne of the Father. God has never rejected my worship when I sing to Him in my brokenness. In fact, that is when I most profoundly experience His sweet love that heals and reshapes my brokenness, molding me anew for His glorious purpose.

The truly intimate worshiper who knows God in these last days will be capable of influencing and instructing the masses. The goal of the word of God is to produce intimate and true worshipers of God. This is why we unite as a body to worship God in unity.

Prayer and the word of God take us to a more intimate and deeper communion with God, making us intimate worshipers who worship in freedom with revelation and understanding. This kind of worship opens the heavens and takes us directly into our King's chambers.

The goal of God's word is to produce intimate and true worshipers of God. That is why we come together as a body to worship God in unity.

Speaking with God (prayer) and reading His love letter (the Bible) helps us to know more about the God who gave everything so that we may live a life without guilt or condemnation. This turns us into intimate worshipers who worship in freedom with revelation and understanding. This type of worship opens the heavens and takes us directly into the chambers of our King.

"*So let us come boldly to the throne of our gracious God. There we will receive his mercy, and we will find grace to help us when we need it most.*" (Hebrews 4:16, NLT)

Worship with confidence!

Chapter 19

The Difference between Worship and Singing

If you can talk, you can sing. Anybody can sing even if they don't know how to hold a tune.

Since God is the Creator of sound, He deserves to be worshiped with our musical sounds. When we sing without a worshiping heart, it's just making noise. It's not a pleasant sound for the Lord. But when you sing while worshiping in spirit and truth, then you are worshiping Him.

When you worship, you are not thinking of yourself or doing it as a show like a "Hollywood" artist. You are not doing it because it's part of the liturgy of the service. You are not bored and do not think of something else when you are singing.

When you engage in worship, you are actively contemplating and meditating upon the profound message conveyed by the lyrics in the song. You are singing as if you wrote that song, which means something to you. It's an offering you are giving to the Lord. You are using the air that comes from your lungs and mouth to worship your Creator, the one who gave you the air and your breath. "Let everything that has breath praise the LORD!" (Psalm 150:6 NKJV).

When you worship, you mean what you sing, and you sing what you mean. Your mind is all there, present, and not back home or distracted with other worries. It is completely surrendered and focused on Him.

When you are singing only, you can be singing, yet your mind can be totally disconnected from what the message in the song is about; you are just singing a tune. That's all. When you worship, you love the One you are singing to and all the brethren singing as one body. When you worship, you thank the Lord for His love and powerful works. It becomes a romantic session where there is romancing back and forth between you and the Lord.

I remember singing a praise song in my home church when I was twelve. Everyone was singing this song over and over and over. As I was singing that praise song, the Lord spoke to me strongly as in a rebuke and asked me, "Do you know what you are singing? Or are you just singing without understanding the words?"

That was the first time I paused to meditate on what we were singing. When I started singing the praise song again, it was a completely different experience. I could sing, feel and understand the words in that praise song. From that day on, I sang differently. I meant what I sang, and I sang what I meant. As the scriptures say, "So what shall I do? I will pray with my spirit, but I will also pray with my understanding; I will sing with my spirit, but I will also sing with my understanding." (1 Corinthians 14:15 (NIV)

Chapter 20

The Importance of Waiting and Surrendering in Worship

"Our failure to make room for the glory in our services is the most common reason that the glory is not seen and experienced in church after church across America and around the world. I believe that most of the necessary elements are in place, but we simply don't give God a chance. We don't make room for Him to work. We don't make room for the glory."

—Ruth Ward Heflin

It is crucial to wait and surrender in our worship; in this way, we make space for the glory of God to enter among us. He is the Sovereign King with eternal supreme dominion. He should dominate our worship services. We know that when His glory enters a place, nothing can stay the same; everything is transformed. The Father seeks worshippers in spirit and truth who surrender completely. The best act of worship you can offer to God is by giving Him your complete will. To wait and surrender involves giving Him our will.

I've always served God, and as we moved from one state to another, I attended various churches over the years. I've noticed that in some of these churches, time is consistently valued more highly than the Holy Spirit.

I understand that people have obligations in their daily lives that require them to work, but was that the purpose of God creating us? So, we can run behind a clock all day and weeklong? When does it stop?

One thing I remember about worship from my revelation of heaven is that in heaven, there is no way to measure time and that sometimes Jesus would speak to me without opening His mouth. He would just transmit to my spirit His words and revelation. We cannot confine God to a set of preferences for our comforts or pleasures.

Does not the Bible tell us in Matthew 6:33 these things dominate the thoughts of unbelievers, but our heavenly Father already knows all our needs? Doesn't it say that we must seek the kingdom of God above all else and live righteously, and He will give us everything we need? Does not it say that we should not worry about tomorrow, for tomorrow will bring its own worries and that today's trouble is enough for today?

If this is what God says, why are we always running our lives by a clock, especially when we worship God? Even in the service, isn't the word of God supposed to be about teaching us to become worshipers of God? Then why do we put our worship on a timer?

I have always heard the people of God say they want revival, but when revival tries to come, it is faced with a stop sign because the god Time says so. Really?

I notice that people are willing to wait long hours if it has to do with money or fame or something selfish, but they are not willing to wait and surrender in God's presence during worship.

I used to be invited to lead worship at events such as conventions or pastor's gatherings, but as I was ushering in the presence and just as the presence was becoming stronger and truly powerful, the main leader of the event would stop it, because the program (the god of Time) must go on. What if God wants to come in and bring transformation? What if this breaks the program and men's agenda? But then we want revival? Absolutely false. We don't really want revival when we don't surrender our clocks to God. God will never submit to our clocks; our clocks must submit to God's agenda and timing.

It takes time to decontaminate, declutter, and refocus on God's goodness and love, especially when we come together as the body of Christ. This cannot happen when we are in a rush all the time because our god clock is yelling, "Time is up!" We were not created to live like this, behind the clock. Our creation had a purpose, and it was not to run behind our alarm clocks.

All the great men in the Bible waited for long periods to receive God's orders. The book of Psalms is filled with *selah* moments. We must have those selah moments, not just in the secret place, but also when we come together as the body of Christ.

Have you ever wondered what could happen in our services if we surrendered our clocks to God? Every minute spent before Him In prayer and worship is time multiplied for our future and destiny.

When we worship without reserve and the restrictions of time, great things happen, and revival could be the result. Why? Because the time is here now when true worshipers will worship the Father in spirit and truth, and especially because the Father is looking for those who will worship Him in spirit and in truth (see John 4:23–24).

Those who worship in spirit and truth are the ones who surrender their agendas and clocks to Him in exchange for His glorious presence and power. This is important because our bodies and minds were not created to live in a continuous rush, always being busy. We were created to live in continuous communion with God, remaining in Him, because apart from Him, we cannot function. It's like a dead cellphone—no connection, no power, and as a result, dysfunction, and uselessness. God's word is clear about this: "...Not by might, nor by power, but by my Spirit, says the LORD of hosts." (Zechariah 4:6, ESV) The Spirit of the Lord is our fountain of power.

When we wait and surrender in worship to Him, individually and corporately, we align ourselves with God's will and original plan. It takes faith to stop and wait; it may even be seen as a waste of time. However, I assure you that it is the best investment of time, benefiting not just you but all who surround you. We accomplish more in God's Presence than with our own efforts. As the word of God says,

"Abide in me, and I in you. As the branch cannot bear fruit by itself, unless it abides in the vine, neither can you, unless you abide in me. I am the vine; you are the branches. Whoever abides in me and I in him, he it is that bears much fruit, for apart from me you can do nothing." (John 15:4–5, ESV)

Furthermore, according to His word, we are called to "Be still in the presence of the Lord and wait patiently for him to act" (Psalm 37:7). Similarly, we're reminded to "Wait patiently for the Lord and be brave and courageous; [and again emphasizes to us] "Yes, wait patiently for the Lord" (Psalm 27:14). Despite these clear directives, why do we often find it challenging to abide by them? Why is it hard to wait and surrender our time? The answer to this question can go in a thousand directions. It all boils down to the condition of our hearts and how spiritually hungry we are. However, if we earnestly desire a spiritual awakening in our land and beyond, it is important to learn and master the discipline of waiting patiently and surrendering to God's perfect timing.

How is it that time in the theater seems short, but in God's house, it seems like a long time for some? Or how is it that our heavenly Father's business seems like an eternity for some, but in their own businesses, time flies? These questions are worth pondering and can prompt some introspection to examine our hearts before the Lord. God is the architect of time and times within eternity; He is the God of the Sabbath. Therefore, embracing patience entails surrendering to His sovereign rhythm instead of imposing our own haste or agendas onto His plans.

Ultimately, surrendering to and waiting on the Lord requires denying ourselves, taking up our cross, and following His lead. We should be wherever He is; wherever He goes, there we should also be. He has said that if we lose our life for His sake, then we will find our true life. (See Matthew 16:24–25)

If we are to be of any use to God in bringing people to His increased, glorious, and holy presence, it's important to surrender everything in submission to Him, with humility, and actively feed the holy fire within us each day. This will allow us to minister from the AUTHORIZED fire of God.

Chapter 21

How to Release the Songs of the Father

In order to find the song of the Father, there must first be a state of brokenness and a willingness to deny ourselves, take up His cross, suffer for His cause, and obey Him at all costs. I am aware that this message is not widely accepted. I get it. My spirit knows it is the way, even though my flesh doesn't like it.

Every time you are willing to suffer for His cause and obey the Lord, the Father writes a song about you in a scroll, which is released to you at the assigned time as you press on and pursue it with all your heart.

During your worship, don't be afraid to navigate beyond the PowerPoint lyrics. Don't limit yourself to the written words; instead, delve deeper into the river as it grows through your worship. As you continue with a hungry heart into this river's flow, it will become impossible to control. The Holy Spirit will take over, and the miraculous will be unleashed. The song of the Father will start to flow without hindrance, and His glory will be enthroned in your midst. This can continue to grow as deep and powerful as your hunger drives you to go.

Sadly, many times it is at this point where humans think it's enough, and they want to stop the flow of the river. The god, timeclock, is dictating the service and has no tolerance for this kind of intensity of God's manifested presence. Nonetheless, I am a witness that although our church service program was interrupted by the Spirit many times, it was during those times when we saw massive deliverance, healings, family restoration, tears of repentance, salvations, and many more testimonies of God encounters that brought spiritual transformation. Often, there was no sermon preached, but instead, there were prophetic declarations, words of knowledge, and prayer for the people. The word of God became demonstrated by the work of the Holy Spirit. As the Apostle Paul said, '...my message and my preaching were not in persuasive words of wisdom, but in demonstration of the Spirit and of power, so that your faith would not rest on the wisdom of men, but on the power of God.' (1 Corinthians 2:4–5, NASB95)

Why put God in a religious box? He is God and can do whatever He wishes in our worship services. Aren't our worship services for Him? Why are some people so worried about their agendas? Can you imagine what could happen in our nation if all churches allowed God to be God and take control of our corporate worship services?

I know this might make some of my brethren uncomfortable, but remember how Jesus made many religious people very uncomfortable? I used to be one of them, and I understand it's a process for some. It was for me as well. However, I wish I had had a book like this to help me back then. If there was one, I never saw it. So, you are blessed because you get to have this resource.

It is time to let go and go deeper. We need more of God, more than ever before. There is so much more God wants to show us. I am glad you picked up this book because this is a sign you are advancing in this. Prepare and be willing to go beyond your religious, human-made traditions. This will be the most exciting spiritual journey of your life!

NEW SONG NEW REVELATION OF HIMSELF

When Israel crossed the Red Sea, Miriam sang a new song of celebration for their victory. This was a powerful, new revelation of God's mighty power. They had never seen God in action in this way. They were in awe! This released a new song in Miriam's heart and the people of Israel!

According to most Bible scholars and standard translations, the specific phrase or concept of "Singing a new Song" appears approximately eleven times in the Bible. Miriam sang a new song. Mary sang a new song. Moses sang a new song. David composed at least 75 of the 150 psalms in the Bible, but perhaps he wrote many more. No one ever heard what he sang when he was tending the sheep.

In both the Old and New Testaments, there are several instances where individuals or groups are described as singing a new song or songs of praise, often in response to God's actions or revelation.

IN THE OLD TESTAMENT:

1. Moses and the Israelites sang a song of praise and deliverance to the Lord after crossing the Red Sea. (see Exodus 15)
2. Miriam, the sister of Aaron and Moses, led the women in song and dance with a timbrel in her hand celebrating the Lord's glorious triumph. (see Exodus 15:20-21)

3. Deborah and Barak sang a song of victory after the defeat of the Canaanite army. (See Judges 5)
4. Many of the Psalms are attributed to King David, who was known for his psalms and songs to God. (see Psalm 33:3; 40:3; 96:1; 98:1; 144:9; 149:1)
5. Asaph and the Sons of Korah, who were Levitical musicians, are credited with writing several Psalms, which are essentially songs or hymns.

IN THE NEW TESTAMENT:

1. Mary, the mother of Jesus, sang the Magnificat, a song of praise and thanksgiving to God, upon visiting Elizabeth. (see Luke 1:46-55)
2. Zechariah, the father of John the Baptist, sang a prophetic song known as the Benedictus after his son's birth. (see Luke 1:67-79)
3. Angels, a multitude of heavenly hosts praised God with song at the birth of Jesus. (see Luke 2:13-14)
4. The 144,000 are described as singing a new song before the throne of God, the four living creatures and the elders. (see Revelation 5:9-10 and 14:3)

These examples encompass various situations and experiences where singing a new song was demonstrated with individual expressions of gratitude and praise, collective rejoicing in God's deliverance and the utterance of prophetic messages.

To sing a new song does not mean despising the old songs but rather singing them with the new wine of God's revelatory presence. Every song is a testimony of a point in your life when you experienced God in a new way and therefore got a new revelation of who He is. This birthed a new song in your heart. God is always creating new things; it is in His nature to create continually. How exciting is this! Words have power, and a song is a powerful declaration with an anointed sound from your mouth that can cause a change in the spiritual realm and atmosphere around you (see Proverbs 18:21).

A song is not supposed to be for entertainment; otherwise, it will be more for the lust of the flesh. It is supposed to be an encounter with God, an experience that will draw you closer to God's love and power so you can grow in your relationship with Him. I promise you that discovering this can make you addicted to His presence. Once you are a carrier of His presence, you will also carry a new song with new revelation in your heart. A new prophetic and anointed song releases a fresh understanding of both God's glorious nature and your significance to Him.

Everyone carries a new song of the Father when they obey and deny themselves to follow Him. This begins with a spirit of thanksgiving and a hunger for His presence and wisdom. Most songs mentioned in the Bible differ significantly from the format and structure of the songs we are familiar with today. They often continued endlessly; when they stopped, it would be called a selah moment. Selah indicates a pause in the text. This pause might be for reflection on what has been said, for meditation, or for a musical interlude, especially in the context of the Psalms being used as hymns. It is thought to underscore or emphasize the significance of the statement that precedes it. It's akin to saying, 'Pause and think about this.' The word Selah appears 71 times in the Psalms and three times in Habakkuk, underscoring its importance as a spiritual practice for us as worshipers. Imagine how much more impactful services could become if we incorporated the practice of pausing, waiting, and reflecting on His word, within an unrushed, contemplative atmosphere saturated with His glorious Presence.

The bride should serenade the bridegroom with songs that

are more intimate and romantic. It's important to maintain that spark for our bridegroom. For some worshippers, these terms of intimacy might be unfamiliar, yet they are rooted in biblical principles. Scripture describes the heavenly welcome feast as a wedding feast, symbolizing us as the bride. We should embody the passion of a bride deeply in love with her bridegroom Jesus, mirroring the bride in the Song of Solomon. Our worship should reflect this, filled with new and intimate songs.

These songs are not about being age-appropriate or catering to the specific styles of either the young or the old. The paramount concern is that the Almighty I Am receives all the attention, honor, and glory He deserves. Such songs promote worship that is solely focused on Him, characterized by a surrendered heart that seeks only His delight. Worship is supposed to be for Him, not for our delight tailored to our own pleasure or preferences. We ought to always expect and desire a new song from the Lord, for heaven resounds with melodies from the throne. The Father wants us to sing a new songs inspired by the ever-evolving harmonies that surround His holy Throne.

Chapter 22

A Key to the Throne & Presence of God

The Samaritan woman was stuck in her culture's religious box, so Jesus declared this truth to her: "You Samaritans know very little about the one you worship...But the time is coming—indeed, it's here now—when true worshipers will worship the Father in spirit and in truth. The Father is looking for those who will worship him that way. For God is Spirit, so those who worship him must worship in spirit and in truth." (John 4:22–24)

The blood of Christ has made it possible for us to worship the Father. Without the blood of Christ, we could not adore Him. But the Father *seeks* worshipers who adore Him in spirit and truth. Three reasons for this are, first, we were created to worship Him; second, because worship is key for the last day's revival; and third, worship is the language of victory from heaven. But to worship effectively, we must have more revelation of who He is to us and who we are to Him. We must know God and be known by God intimately. This is accomplished through a continuous search for His presence in the secret place and searching the Scriptures earnestly.

As we delve deeper into this revelation, we can worship God with a profound understanding in spirit and truth. It can be challenging to worship someone you don't truly know or have a desire to know. This type of worship is relationship-based. It begins by recognizing and acknowledging that Jesus is the Son of God, your personal Savior and Redeemer. He is your Deliverer and your Healer, but He is so much more than that. God desires this more than we can ever desire it. Don't stop there; keep nurturing your relationship with God every day. This is what worshiping Him is all about! To truly get to know Him, and Love Him with all our heart, mind, soul and strength. Worshiping Him is loving Him wholeheartedly.

Instruments and songs are just tools, but the worship of our hearts is not a tool. Worship is a lifestyle of intimacy with God, total surrender to Him, and absolute and immediate obedience to Him. Worship is the reason we were created. We were created to worship the King of kings and Lord of lords with all our existence. We are worshipers from eternity to eternity. The atmosphere of Heaven is created by our sincere and true worship, which is full of revelation and intimacy with Christ (using whatever the tool—musical instruments, singing, dancing, chanting, proclaiming, declaring, etc.). This is where His presence manifests like a river that suddenly floods upon our lives and atmospheres.

Worship is vitally important in releasing the presence of God wherever you are, but for that to happen, we have to lead the way in going deep in our intimacy with the beautiful presence of God. *Where there is no true worship, there is no manifested presence of God.* This is because our worship is a sign of gratitude and thanksgiving, which God requires of us. His presence is manifested, and the Spirit of God operates freely when there is an atmosphere full of praise and gratitude in the people of God.

God tells us in His word that we should not be drunk with wine because that will ruin our lives. Instead, He wants us to "be filled with the Holy Spirit, singing psalms and hymns and spiritual songs among [our brethren], and making music to the Lord in [our] hearts." More than this, we are to "give thanks for everything to God the Father in the name of our Lord Jesus Christ" (Ephesians 5:18–20). The Lord commands us through His word to "Enter his gates with thanksgiving; go into his courts with praise. Give thanks to him and praise his name" (Psalm 100:4).

I want to make it clear that worship does not save us. Christ has already saved us. But worship is essential for our communion with Him, which signifies our maturity level in our relationship with God. True worship is necessary as we continue saturating our spirit with His presence. The Father is present wherever there is genuine worship because He is looking for genuine worshipers who approach God with a humble heart.

Another important reason is that the Father can entrust the nations to this kind of worshiper. He loves those who love Him (see Proverbs 8:17, John 14:21). Worship in heaven is continuous because it is necessary that those who are there worship the Father continuously. Imagine a quiet heaven with no one worshiping the Father. I don't think so! Worship is connected directly to His presence.

When there is worship in spirit and truth, the result inevitably would be His glorious presence is manifested. Take time during the day to worship God with or without tools, trusting that worship is about your heart bowed before Him more than the tools you use. Your mouth is a trumpet of worship. Use it to bring down the glory of God. Tell God how much you love Him and how beautiful He is to you. Carry and release the presence of God wherever you go today!

Chapter 23

Struck Down, but Not Destroyed

Some of our most powerful worship comes when we are broken. As Steffany Gretzinger says, "If your heart is broken, you need to dance."[1]

You have no idea how much I've had to go through to write this book. There has been a spiritual war against me since I began writing this book from day one. Why? Because true worship is a threat to the demonic side of the spiritual world. The enemy tried to kill my worshiping heart a few times during the writing of this book. My heart was beaten and bruised by the ministry, financial crisis, health challenges, and worries of life. I allowed anger into my heart, and my faith was weakened. I was struck down for a moment. Anger is the worst enemy of a worshiper.

I battled with the anger I had allowed into my heart for about a year and a half. Although I decided to forgive those who hurt me, I still dealt with pain and anger. I loved God, and my heart wanted God more than anything. But anger and disappointment were in the way. Don't let this happen to you! It is spiritually lethal if we don't turn away from it. And it is profoundly challenging, if not impossible, to worship God with an angry heart.

At one point, I felt that my heart had become dull, so I could not worship in the same way. I could not write a song as easily as before when it flowed like a river. It was extremely difficult; I began to feel and think about defeat and failure. I went through a depressive period. Fear crippled my life, and I fell into a dull state. I momentarily thought I had lost my edge and creativity.

My relationship with God became dry, and I felt like I had fallen into a ditch and could not get myself out. It was taking me lots of work and effort even to function. I felt exhausted. Suddenly, I lost my sense of direction and purpose in life. No wonder the word of God says, "And "don't sin by letting anger control you." Don't let the sun go down while you are still angry, for anger gives a foothold to the devil." (Ephesians 4:26–27)

Allowing anger to take root in your heart can have profound spiritual and physical consequences, impacting not only your connection with God but also your overall well-being. It gives the devil a dangerous foothold in your life.

ADDICTED TO WORRY

My heart felt anxious and worried about everything, especially our finances. All these worries were weighing me down. Like the word says, "Anxiety in a man's heart weighs him down, but a good word makes him glad" (Proverbs 12:25 ESV).

Through all this, I received a new understanding of why Jesus said, "Watch out! Don't let your hearts be dulled by carousing and drunkenness, and by the worries of this life. Don't let that day catch you unaware" (Luke 21:34).

God puts the word *drunkenness* in the same verse as

worries of this life. Many people drink to forget about their problems or temporarily feel happy. This may be why bars have signs announcing, "Happy hour." It is evident here that people are looking for happiness, peace, and joy. It struck me, however, that God mentions the worries of life as something that makes your heart dull. The dictionary defines the word *dull* as:

Not sharp; blunt: a dull knife, causing boredom; tedious; uninteresting, not lively or spirited; not bright, intense, or clear; dim: a dull sound, slow in motion or action; not brisk; sluggish, mentally slow; lacking brightness of mind; somewhat stupid; obtuse, lacking keenness of perception in the senses or feelings; insensible; unfeeling.[2]

This is pretty serious stuff. I realized that, just as drunkenness is an addiction, worry is equally an addiction. I was addicted to worry, and as a result, my heart became dull.

The opposite of worrying is a heart overflowing with the Spirit and life, a joyful heart that is continually singing psalms, hymns, and spiritual songs, making music to the Lord, and giving thanks to God for everything.

I understood in more depth this important gem principle that surprised me about the contrast between drunkenness and being filled with the Holy Spirit, as it says in Ephesians 5:18–20. I was also able to see how the worries of this life could take root in our hearts and not permit the word of God to affect us. Jesus describes this in the parable of the Sower, saying, "The thorns represent others who hear God's word, but all too quickly the message is crowded out by the worries of this life... so no fruit is produced" (Mark 4:18–19).

So, what are we to do to overcome worry? We are to praise God with thankfulness and be intentional in trusting Him. "When I am afraid, I put my trust in you. In God, whose word I praise, in God I trust; I shall not be afraid. What can flesh do to me?" (Psalm 56:3–4 ESV).

I learned to be ever-aware that nobody cares for me more than God. He wants me to exchange my anxieties for His care to regain sober-mindedness and be watchful against the schemes of the enemy. Only in this way can we resist the devil and stand firm in our faith (see 1 Peter 5:6–11).

OVERCOME BY JOY

When we follow the process God gives us and trust Him to take care of the things that fill us with worry, we will stay filled with the Holy Spirit. Instead of being intoxicated by worry, which can ruin our lives by dulling our hearts, we can choose to be intoxicated with the Holy Spirit. He fills us with joy and confidence in Him.

Knowing this, can you imagine living a carefree life from a worshiping heart? Try to imagine it. Imagine that, instead of being filled with anger, regret, or concerns, you are filled with praise, positive thoughts, creativity, joy, peace, innovation, enthusiasm, power, and purpose that leads us to help others. More than that, we would have laughter, a sense of security, confidence, life, love, and even prosperity.

This is the life God invites us to enjoy with Him. It is the life of being a true worshiper. This may be why God says, "Guard your heart above all else, for it determines the course of your life" (Proverbs 4:23). Our heart is the deepest essence of our being. It is like a treasure chest that stores either good treasures or bad things. If our hearts are not right, our mouths will not produce and release pure worship to God. Therefore, it will not be able to bring forth the breath of God and the songs of the Father. Jesus taught us that what comes out of a person's mouth flows from the heart and affects our life.

When I wake up in the morning, I first go to His presence and make it my home for a few hours, spending time with

Daddy, then I go to work. I notice that things turn out better that day because I gave Him priority and the due respect and honor He deserves.

Let me explain what I mean. When I am in His presence, I am home with my Daddy. When I study His word, I am home with my Daddy.

His Presence and His word are home for my spirit. I feel at home when I spend time with Him. He gives me peace, love, and so much happiness. He is my place of comfort, my place of love, and my place of peace.

Worshiping God is like medicine to our minds, soul, and spirit. When you worship God, you take your mind off yourself and put it on God. You are training your mind to stay focused on God and sending a message to your brain that God is a better thought. God designed your brain to respond to Him and His presence.

Even when you speak in tongues, your brain might not understand it, but the spirit of your mind will understand it completely. When you speak in tongues, you connect with heaven's language, and your brain receives the joy and the freedom to think forward and clearly. I believe worship gives us the vision to see ahead and hope to believe wholeheartedly, bringing joy to our hearts.

OUR FIRST CALL IS TO WORSHIP

Why was Jesus tempted in the desert regarding worship, and what is it with worship? The devil wanted Jesus's worship, and he wants yours, too. He has always wanted the worship of the universe for himself. His arrogant, prideful, and jealous heart wished to rule in place of God, which is why he lost all he had. He persistently seeks worship that doesn't rightfully belong to him, and regrettably, many individuals, including

Christians, unintentionally end up worshiping the adversary of their souls.

Our primary calling from God is to worship Him as our Lord and King; it's the very purpose for which you were created. As a worshiper, you and I are invaluable for these last days. You become an important conduit of heaven the minute you start worshiping the Lord in spirit and truth.

The Father is seeking those kinds of worshipers, but why? What is it about worship that is vital for the Father to find them? He has myriads and myriads of angels in heaven who worship Him eternally, so He does not need more worshipers. This means He must be looking for something more significant, not because He needs it, but because we need it. It is crucial that we act in accordance with our calling, which is to worship the Lord and be channels of His fire of revival on this earth. The Father can trust those true worshipers and, therefore, can use them as the conduits of His mighty power and fire to bring His revival and spiritual awakening on earth.

The apostle Paul, in Romans 12, reminds us that offering our bodies to God is a way of honoring Him for His blessings and that true worship involves presenting ourselves as living and holy sacrifices to the Lord. It goes beyond mere music; worship extends into the transformation of our character and renewing our minds. Through this kind of worship, we gain insight into God's will for our lives, which is good, pleasing, and perfect. (see Romans 12:1–2).

While we may face moments of adversity and feel struck down, we should remember that we are never truly defeated or destroyed as long as we have God on our side. We might be struck down, but as we worship the Lord, He will raise us higher than ever before for His glory and honor! No matter how difficult or painful it may be when you are struck down, you must worship and dance, even with whatever little strength you have left, for in our weakness, He can reveal His strength to us and manifest His glory through us. It is during these times that we can come to truly understand who He is and how deeply He cares for us. Worshiping God in Brokenness while we are struck down is the most exuberant sacrifice of worship, we can ever give God. He delights in this kind of worship, and He is greatly moved by it. Make a mental stairway and climb above your situation up to that heavenly place where your worship will flow unhindered. Miracles will happen at this level. Unhindered worship is deliverance to your soul.

So, let this be a reminder to keep worshiping, regardless of any obstacles or discouragement that may come your way. Don't let anyone or anything hinder your worship, ever!

As we conclude this chapter, let's seal this moment with a heartfelt prayer:

> Father, in Jesus Name I come before you with a heart full of gratitude and trust. Just as the psalmist prayed, I too call upon your Name, and I know that you will answer. You have freed me from my fears, and I know that those who look to you for help will be radiant with joy in your presence and no shadow of shame will darken their face, for you are my refuge. In my moments of desperation, I cry out to you, and I am comforted to know that you always listen and save me from my troubles. Like the angel of the LORD who surrounds and defends those who fear you, I feel your protective presence in my life.
>
> Through Jesus, I offer a sacrifice of praise, openly professing your holy Name. I praise you with all my being and remember your countless benefits. You are the forgiver of sins and the healer of diseases. You

redeem my life from despair and crown me with love and compassion. You satisfy my deepest desires with goodness, renewing my spirit like the eagle's soaring flight.

Thank you, Lord, for your boundless grace and blessings. May my life be a continual offering of praise to you, for you are worthy of all honor and worship.

In Jesus' name, Amen.

- Scripture references:
- Psalm 34:4-7
- Hebrews 13:15
- Psalm 103:1-5

Chapter 24

The Tones of The Throne Will Cost You

Everything that is going on in this world right now is about one thing: Who will worship whom. We know what happened when Jesus was tempted during His forty-day fast. Satan said to Jesus, "All this I will give you ... if you will bow down and worship me." But then Jesus said to him, "Away from me, Satan! For it is written: 'Worship the Lord your God and serve him only.'" (Matthew 4:9–10 NIV).

When my husband and I were pastoring in Faribault, the last two years there, I went through a dark season in my life. Our church had gone through a demonic attack that split the church, and I was heartbroken.

I wrote the following birthday prayer in my journal and at the end of two years of the wilderness and desperation:

Today is my 38th birthday, Lord, and as I reflect on the years that have passed, I want to begin by thanking You for the countless blessings, protection, good health, spiritual growth, and the precious gifts of my two healthy sons and a godly, loving husband.

On this day, however, I find myself in an unusual state. I'm not feeling my best, and I'm uncertain about the cause. Financially, I'm eagerly awaiting a miracle to cover the bills that are due. Spiritually, I yearn for a renewal, a fresh outpouring of Your glory, and a deeper revelation of Your Word. Emotionally, I feel weakened and scarred, seeking Your healing from the wounds that ministry has left in my heart. My chest aches with each breath, and I'm experiencing heightened sensitivity and confusion.

I find myself waiting for You to speak to me or take me to heaven through a supernatural encounter, though I recognize that perhaps it's not Your will for me. [By the way, God answered this prayer a year and a half after I made this prayer].
I know I don't deserve it. I struggle with lots of guilt. My self-doubt and guilt weigh heavily on me, and I wonder if I'm being too hard on myself.

While my earlier dreams have been fulfilled, it feels that I'm in need of a new dream, perhaps one where I write and sing new songs from heaven that I've never heard before, and even record them in an album [God answered this prayer a year and a half after, in an album called The Father's Songs*]. Perhaps I could write books that would bless others' lives and at the same time that* *this may provide for my family, but I'm not certain.* [This prayer was answered by God, giving me seven books, including this one, with more on the way] *Despite my struggles, I know that You are with me, and I understand that this may be a test of my faith.*

I confess that I have lost some of my passion for the ministry, perhaps my level of dependence on You has diminished. Lord, I beg You, have mercy, and teach me your way now, I need your guidance, love, mercy, revelation and so much more. At this time, I feel as if God has left me, even though I know He is here by faith, but I don't see it clearly at this moment. Please God do something. I don't want another year to be the same. Father, take me to a new place in my walk with You and deepen my understanding of who You are [God answered my heart desire five months after this prayer]. *I'm asking You for this with the little strength I have left in me.*

Perhaps I am not asking in the right way. Please, Holy Spirit, I ask you to intercede for me before the Father, for His mercy and for the desire of my heart on my birthday. I have prayed for this since last year for a new and crystal-clear revelation about You, my King and Lord. You know I am trying with the little strength I have left. Remember that I am but dust, I am here today and tomorrow I am no more. I will be of no used to you if I get all I am asking from you when I'm in heaven. It's now that I desire to experience Your inheritance while on earth. I don't think that I'm asking for too much or something outside of Your will. May You fulfill Your promises, for Your Word is powerful and true. As Jesus taught, when we ask in His name, we receive.

I know you want to reveal Yourself to me and give me what I need more than I desire it. Do something remarkable with my life don't want to live a meaningless life nor waste the rest of my life. please sweet Father Jesus, and Holy Spirit.

Waiting, Your daughter. Thanks for creating me, January 14.

I wrote this in my journal, providing context for this prayer, explaining that it was written on my birthday during one of the darkest periods of my life.

The next morning after I wrote this letter to God, I tuned in to TBN and received a direct word from the Lord and encouragement for my situation. I realized that I wasn't the only one going through this dark season in life. The church, in general, was going through a dark and unclear time. It was a season of re-identifying ourselves with Christ, learning who we are in Him, and learning to put Him first and not let any things of life get in the way.

That morning, I asked myself, *Where am I in my life?* I had worked very hard for nine years in our ministry in Faribault. Before that, I worked with our district youth, traveling all over the country, giving beyond my strength, and always going the extra mile, sometimes on empty. I realized that I had done many things with my strength when only in His strength and power would I be able to complete this journey in ministry with my husband.

The next morning after I wrote this letter, I heard a great man and prophet of God, John Paul Jackson, speaking of his dark times. The questions he made to God and his experience sounded just like mine. He would look in the mirror and say, "God are you real? Do you really exist? Did you call me to the ministry? Lord, are you really here? Have you really called me to be in this place?"

These were some of the same questions I was asking myself during this dark time. I didn't feel like I even wanted to be there anymore. I thought of other solutions and ways of getting myself out of that situation because my worst rival, my flesh, kept telling me, *This is it; I can't take it anymore.*

I identify with the words of the apostle Paul: Not that I have already obtained it or have already become perfect, but I press on so that I may lay hold of that for which also I was laid hold of by Christ Jesus. Brethren, I do not regard myself as having laid hold of it yet; but one thing I do: forgetting what lies behind and reaching forward to what lies ahead, I press on toward the goal for the prize of the upward call of God in Christ Jesus. Philippians 3:12–14, NASB95

I'm not there yet, but I am pressing on. I haven't accomplished what I want to do for the Lord, but I'm pressing on toward the prize of the upward call of God—I am not giving up! I will start afresh today, the day after my birthday. Every day will be a new day for me, a new fresh start. I will keep trying until I obtain my goal and reward from the Lord Jesus Christ. My life is meaningless unless I press on for what God wants of me. I will not waste my days of life any more on things of this earth. I will not waste my life on things that add no eternal value to my life, my family, or our spiritual family in this world.

I'm sure it'll cost me tears. It's already cost me a lot of tears. I know it will cause me pain and fatigue, as it has in the past. But my goal is to become the woman God wants me to be. I will not stop, even though I sometimes feel like I have no more strength to keep going. Sometimes, I feel like God has left me, although I know deep inside that He has not and will never leave me.

My feelings, my internal rival, tells me things like - God is not listening to you. God has left you. But I know deep inside my heart that the Holy Spirit inside of me is with me. The same one who raised Jesus Christ from the dead is the same one who will lift me up from this dark situation, and He will show me how to trust in Him. He will show me a new revelation of His love, which I so much need. As Ephesians 3:19 says, He will help me to know the love of Christ, which surpasses all knowledge, so that I may be filled with all the fullness of God.

One thing that I want this year is to know the love of Christ. I want to learn more about it. I desire to be filled to the fullness of God. I don't want to be a mediocre or an ordinary Christian. I don't want to live a one-size-fits-all gospel. I want all the fullness of God.
Did you hear me? God, I want the fullness that comes from You! I want to be filled up completely!

My emotions need the fullness of God. My mind needs the fullness of God. My heart needs the fullness of God. I need to be completely filled with God. I'm not talking about religiosity. I am not talking about tradition or the old usual church stuff. I need to be filled up completely with the fullness of God's glorious nature. I try to imagine this, and I try to see what it would be like. What would that look like? How would that happen?

However, I'm not going to worry about it because I'm not God, and that is not my burden to bear. That is God's responsibility, for He is well aware of the desires of my heart. My desire is to be filled with His fullness until it overflows, and I believe it is His divine will to grant me this, and my duty is to earnestly seek His fullness.

The Word of God instructs me to seek Him first, to seek all that comes or originates from above first, the Kingdom of God—and assures me that all other things will be added unto me. But the 'how' of it remains a mystery to me. Half of the time, I have no idea what I am doing, except for the certainty than that, I know I am in his will, and I have no intention of straying from it. If He is God, He knows and understands what He is doing, even though I occasionally find myself pondering numerous unanswered questions.

My longing is like the psalmist wrote, "As the deer pants for the water brooks, So my soul pants for You, O God. My soul thirsts for God, for the living God; When shall I come and appear before God? My tears

> have been my food day and night, While they say to me all day long, "Where is your God?" These things I remember, and I pour out my soul within me. For I used to go along with the throng and lead them in procession to the *house of God, With the voice of joy and thanksgiving, a multitude keeping festival."* (Psalm 42:1–4, NASB95)
>
> My flesh is my worst rival. This is the question my flesh asks me many times, *If you are serving God, and if you are in God's will, then why is He not answering your prayers? If He is your God, why has He allowed everything that happened in the last year and a half of your life?*
>
> That is what the inner rival keeps telling me, but as I read the Bible, I understand my walk is not a walk by sight but a walk by faith. The just will live by faith, which is the hardest thing to do. It's hard, but it's not impossible. It is hard for the flesh, but as I align myself with the Holy Spirit through prayer and meditation on His word, I can see that it is not hard if I do it with God's strength. When we try to do things with our own strength, it will not work. I've tried it. It doesn't work.

I wrote this prayer in my journal a year and a half into the two years of darkness I endured. What happened? Our church underwent a devastating split triggered by the distribution of a DVD containing a poisonous teaching, which was given to one of our deacons from an outside source.

Tragically, he consumed the poison and began spreading its influence to others. My husband and I faced numerous distressing circumstances as a result. The stress and anguish caused by betrayal became so unbearable that I had to make multiple visits to the emergency room with heart pain. Strangely, while at church, God's presence would still be mighty as I sang and ministered in my brokenness, but the moment I returned to our home, everything would become dark again.

"YOU DON'T KNOW ME"

As stated in my journal above, I watched John Paul Jackson give a testimony of a similar situation that caught my attention. When I heard his testimony, I could identify with him and realized that many people were going through this. I knelt in the living room next to my computer, listening to soaking worship. In my prayer, I asked God why He had allowed everything to happen and where He was in all of this. I had a lot of unanswered questions.

Suddenly, I heard the voice of God speak so clearly into my spirit.

He said, "You don't know me."

I responded, "What? I don't know You? I've served You all my life. How is it possible that I don't know You?"

He said, "Everything you know about Me has helped you up to this point in your life, but you need a new revelation of who I am and who you are in Me to go where I am taking you next. You will need to know Me deeper to face what will be ahead of you and where I am taking you."

It was like God saying to me, "You still haven't come to know and understand the width, length, height, and depth of who I am and of My love for you, which surpasses your knowledge. You need to be filled with Me to the measure of all My fullness." (See Ephesians 3:17-19)

At that moment, I understood that I only knew Him

through my past experiences and what others had told me about Him, and that was only to a certain level.

Many times, when we grow up in the Gospel, we are so afraid to err in the scriptures or even to fall into heresy that we are afraid to go deeper and totally closed to anything new God wants to do in us. We get to being so careful that we close the doors to the Holy Spirit's new revelation. We are afraid of any new revelation, so we close up and become a museum of the Gospel. This leaves us orphaned in our Christian faith because we stop growing in the knowledge and revelation of God.

While still on my knees, I had a God-aligned moment. The computer changed my music, and a new CD started playing. I had not realized that my husband had purchased this CD and loaded it on the computer. The CD was from the same prophet I had seen on television, John Paul Jackson, and on the CD were 365 names of God. Suddenly, all my attention was fixed on that CD because I didn't even know I had it. The music started saying:

I am 365 names, characteristics, and attributes of God.

I am the God who shows wonders.

I am the Lord, and my voice is powerful and full of majesty.

I am wisdom.

I am omniscient.

I am Jehovah Rapha[1]

Suddenly, I got an *Aha* moment!

As the CD went on, it felt like a blindfold, or scales were coming off my eyes and the dark cloud gradually dissipated for each name and quality of the Great I Am mentioned. It seemed as though God timed everything so that I suddenly realized and understood how enormous my God was.

I exclaimed, "Wow! God is really, really gigantic and huge; I was making Him so, so small all this while!"

Suddenly, a veil fell off my eyes, and I immediately realized that I had been serving God with all my heart but with a little revelation of who He is and who I am in Him. I was living my Christian life with past and old revelations about Him, things I had learned from past experiences, and other people's experiences since childhood. Sure, I did have awesome experiences in the past with God, but they had become the old wine. I had not learned any fresh or new revelation about who God really is or who I am in Him. God is a personal God who wanted to reveal Himself to me deeper. He was calling me deeper and He was answering my birthday prayer.

A NEW BEGINNING

As a result, from that day forward, the period of night or darkness vanished from my life, and a new journey began. I was so hungry to know more about who God is and who I am in Him that I started searching the scriptures from Genesis to Revelation to find all the names and attributes of God. By the end of my study, I had found a thousand names and attributes of God.

My worship went to a whole new level. It was filled with a new revelation about God and who I am to Him. When we do not have this revelation, we only know what others have told us or we rely on our old experiences of things we lived through ten or twenty years ago. Even a revelation from a year ago can be ineffective if it has become cold and stale, or if you are still depending on it in your spiritual life without keeping it fresh and growing deeper in that revelation. Do we eat meat and bread from a year ago? Absolutely not! We always like to eat fresh meat and bread. Besides, it's not even healthy to eat old, expired food, right?

God is always doing new things because He is a creative God.

With everything that was happening that year, 2020, I needed to finish this book Pronto! I returned to the thousand names and attributes of God and got over two hundred more, making the total over one thousand two hundred names and attributes of God. If we can learn three a day and a hundred a month, we will know God one thousand two hundred times deeper by the end of this year. This can be used as a daily way to escape the stresses and difficulties of life. Just pick a few names and attributes of God and delve into them as a river that will refresh your soul.

Chapter 25

Revival Worshipers' Commissioning

In the year 2020, while I was completing the first version of this book, many alarming things were happening, from violent riots, burning buildings, looting, Covid-19, and financial crisis to turmoil in America and around the world. With all this happening, it is easy to lose focus on the main thing—God. When you lose your focus, fear can set in and paralyze you. This paralyzing fear inhibits, or even blocks, you from going forward into the marvelous destiny God has for you and through you.

When everything gets too noisy, you cannot focus on anything, turn everything off, find solitude, and then worship. We need to bring the Father's songs to the world now more than ever. The life-giving breath of the Father is what we need. The tones around the throne, saturated with God's presence, are essential in this world.

God needs you and me to bring His mighty presence into this chaotic world. His presence is all we need. It might sound too simple, but this is the absolute truth. There is no other, all-powerful presence in the universe that is somehow mightier than our God. We came from His presence; we shall go back to our original home—to His presence. In His presence, there is this unspeakable peace, joy, healing, hope, deliverance, salvation, transformation, prosperity, innovation, restoration, wisdom, and the list goes on.

God is calling you to bring His songs of deliverance, the songs of His breath. God needs conduits of His glory. We—the worshipers, His bride, His church—are the ones to bring His glory through our worship. Let's bring this worship in spirit and truth to the ends of the earth. Let's fill the earth with the songs of the Father. Let's bring our worship outside of the four walls of the church.

Let's make God known to the people of the world as we release and declare the names and attributes of God over our cities. Let's set our cities on fire with our revival worship through the fire of the Holy Spirit. Let's bring a worship that is wholehearted, Spirit-led, fresh, intimate, deep, prophetic, passionate, liberating, and saturated in His presence with pure and surrendered hearts. This is the revival worship of the last days that the Father desires, as stated in John 4:23–24.

Let's go and fill the earth with His glory through our devoted, intimate worship. Enter your mission field, the world. Go under the bridges, the beaches, and your back yard. Go to the disaster areas, and visit the shopping malls. Go to the parks and the streets. Go outside the church and start releasing *the Father's songs* into those atmospheres.

While I'm reviewing this book, I've seen that the Spirit of God is raising intimate worshippers of the Father, and gradually the Father's songs will envelop this earth. The greatest revival we have ever seen is approaching, filled with the fire of His holiness and glorious Presence.

Start in your home. Start by getting to know at least three names and attributes of God daily. Each week you will learn 21 names and attributes of God, and a hundred each month. If you do this for the next twelve months, you will have learned about twelve hundred names and attributes, significantly increasing your knowledge of who God is.

Make it a goal to get to know God more than ever in your life. Go daily and often into the secret place to meet this wonderful, awesome God you serve. Don't ever give that sacred time of intimacy with God to anything else on your agenda. Nothing is more important than the King of your life. Start by cutting what is unnecessary from your schedule; even if it hurts, do it! Do it for God's glory and the revival that is about to pour into the whole world. Could it be possible that God has been waiting on you to pour out this last-day revival? If you knew this revival depended on your intimacy with God, would you be willing to be that conduit? God is seeking such intimate worshipers.

Don't ever stop worshiping God. Never let anyone stop you from worshiping the Lord. Bow only before the Lord your God. Raise only the name of Jesus Christ. Honor Him and all who are in authority so that nothing can hinder your worship.

Through your worship and standing in that glorious presence of God, *proclaim, declare, and establish* the majestic names and attributes of the Great I Am and His mighty will over the earth. This will release a revival, the glory of God will come upon the earth, and more and more worshipers will be raised throughout the world to give God more and more glory, as He deserves from eternity to eternity, amen.

Let's fill the earth with God's holy presence through our intimate worship of Him!

"Honor the Lord, you heavenly beings; honor the Lord for his glory and strength. Honor the Lord for the glory of his name. Worship the Lord in the splendor of his holiness." (Psalm 29:1–2)

Let's do this today!

PART II

The Glorious Nature of Our God

"And this is the way to have eternal life—
to know you, the only true God, and Jesus Christ,
the one you sent to earth." —John 17:3

Earlier in this book, I shared about my two years of darkness where I often felt the absence of God and how at the end of these two years, God told me, "You don't know me." That experience is behind this Part II of the book.

Earlier in this book, I shared about my two years of darkness where I often felt the absence of God and how at the end of these two years, God told me, "You don't know me." That experience is recounted in Chapter 24.

Throughout the years I served God, from when I was very young to almost ten years in the ministry, I thought I already knew everything I needed to know about God. I lived a life in holiness and pure worship before Him, served Him with all my heart, but I was acting more like a Martha and was missing the most important thing, which was to continue getting to know Him intimately. I was oblivious to this truth, I didn't understand it until the moment when God told me, "You do not know Me."

Through the revelation imparted by the Holy Spirit, I now understand that the moment you come to Christ is only level one in the revelation of who God is. At that point, you get to know, in part, that He is your Savior, Healer, Deliverer, and Restorer, which is indeed enough to fuel your journey for many years.

The issue arises when you remain stagnant at that initial level. The crucial aspect of any level is the progression to the next. Once you reach a new level, the subsequent one becomes the most important. Every revelation of God serves not as a final destination but as a steppingstone to further understanding. God transcends our current knowledge—He is infinitely more, eternally.

Ever since God showed me how important it is for Him that I continually get to know Him, like Paul, I now count all things to be a loss in view of the surpassing value and power of knowing Christ Jesus my Lord (see Philippians 3:7–11).

WHY IS IT IMPORTANT TO KNOW GOD INTIMATELY?

It is important to know God intimately because this is what God desires, and we should too. Intimacy with God authorizes us to do the works of Jesus with His Authority. Ministry is not God and God is not Ministry. Ministry is serving God as a result of our intimacy with God; therefore, Ministry is not the main thing.

Without Him there is no ministry or true worship service. God should always remain the center of it all. When we take our intimacy with God out of the equation of Ministry or our services, we are just using His Name in vain for our own self motives or perhaps for lack of knowledge (see Hosea 4:6).

We will not enter heaven by merely calling Him Lord. Only those who do the will of the Father in heaven will be allowed to enter His Kingdom. And, unless you are united to His will which is—to know who He truly is—He will have to say on that day, "I never knew you; depart from me, you workers of lawlessness" (see Matthew 7:21–23).

We need to truly love and delight in who God is so that God may know us (see 1 Corinthians 8:3).

If we ever want to boast about something, it should be that we understand and know Him, that He is the Lord who practices steadfast love, justice, and righteousness in the earth because it is in these things that the Lord delights (see Jeremiah 9:23-24).

No matter what may or may not happen in your life, remember that Christ is all that matters, and He lives in all of us. This is enough to live a successful godly life (see Colossians 3:10–11). John said it clearly that the way to have eternal life is to know Him, the only true God, and Jesus Christ, the one He sent to this earth (John 17:2–3).

With all this in mind, please make the most of this tool. Take the time to meditate on each of these names and titles of God. Invite the Holy Spirit to reveal them to you personally. As I said, if you do this with just three every day, you will internalize this entire list in one year. Imagine how much deeper and more powerfully you would know the Lord at the end of that time! But the most beautiful thing is this is only the beginning. We cannot stop knowing God after pursuing Him for just one year, but we must press on to know Him until we are face to face with Him in heaven!

FIRST THINGS FIRST

Before we delve into God's names, you need to understand some very important things. Knowing the names of God is going to take a process as your earthly senses are turned into heavenly senses. Your finite mind needs time to process the deep truths of God's nature with His names and attributes. It will be crucial to be intentional by putting a demand on God's power and mercy.

One thing that the woman of the alabaster jar and the woman with the issue of blood, among others, had in common was their persistence and intentional demand for Jesus' power and mercy. What they did was to demand the power and mercy of God, which is the key element to experiencing Him in a more meaningful way. Being intentional in putting a demand on God really means that you truly want this, you're going for it with all your strength, heart, and mind, and you are not giving up. It's like when you intentionally connect your cellphone to the wall outlet to demand that the electricity come into your device. In the same way, you need to intentionally connect to God's names with the Spirit's help so God can give you eyes to contemplate and understand His nature. Oh, Lord, give us eyes to see your glorious nature!

Your spirit needs to download and synchronize each revelational truth of who God is and how much you mean to Him. This is going to take intentional time in His presence. Even when you go through all these names of God, you will realize that it is easy to fall into a state of familiarity or over-comfortability. You must Intentionally go back and revisit His names one by one and give your mind space to process these truths into your spirit. You must know that God wants this more than anyone. If we seek Him with all our heart, He will let us find Him (see Jeremiah 29:13)

God's names are deep in revelation and versatile; they will always get deeper and deeper in revelation. Don't ever be afraid to receive more revelation of God's nature, no matter how much you think you know of the Bible and even the original language of the Bible—you have not arrived yet. There is still much more to discover about our eternal, mighty God. However, we can only do this through the Holy Spirit's help and guidance.

I advise you to go into a quiet place every morning and meditate on one name of God. Then meditate throughout the morning on that one name. At noon, meditate on another name of God. And again, at dinner time, meditate on another name of God for the rest of the evening. Let it permeate your heart and mind. Finally, before bed, take at least ten to fifteen minutes to meditate on the three names you chose that day.

It would be a great investment of time to write in your journal something the Holy Spirit revealed to you through those three names during the day. Do this as a habit, and the Holy Spirit will start to reveal more and more about who God is. Then, when you go through challenging times, trials, or tribulations, you will be able to understand and be aligned with the nature of God and who you have gotten to know Him to be. It will start clicking in; the Holy Spirit will bring just what you need into your mind because you have intentionally deposited God into your spirit.

I must confess that once you are intentional and start doing this, you might not even get past the first name of God for a few days. It happened to me. I began with God's first name, and it literally melted me in tears of awe and reverence as the Lord gave me eyes to see and understand more of this name. It was so profoundly impacting that I could barely process it. I could not go to the second name for more than a week. I just kept pounding on the "I Am Who I Am" name, and it was so deep that I am still processing it because, in my opinion, this one is the deepest in the revelation of God's nature.

As Tim Mackie has said (I am paraphrasing), "I Am Who I Am says a lot of the endless attributes of who God is. First, there is no end to His sovereign names or personal traits. Second, He is as pure as He is. He is always loving, in contrast with we humans, who might sometimes be loving, but sometimes we are not."[1]

WHEN YOU KNOW WHO GOD IS...

It is like putting wood into the fire on the altar. The wood is your intentional effort to know God. When you align and synchronize your mind to God's nature, names, and attributes, you will start getting a deeper revelation of who God is, and your Christian life will be easier to live. You will be able to overcome difficulties easier because now you are clothed with who He is. You are inside of Him, and He is inside of you.

You will get revelation firsthand that, inside of Him, all is good, perfect, pleasing, holy, and pure. You will be able to see life through a different lens—through the lens of God and who He is.

You will experience a paradigm shift. Then fear will have no place in your life because once you know Him, this truth will set you free to believe and trust in Him without any doubt. You will feel secure in how much the God you serve loves and cares for you. You will understand how all-powerful and glorious He is and will never want to live independently of Him. You will not want to ever depend on your strength or understanding for life.

You will understand that everything good and bad that happens has a purpose and a destiny, that inside of the all-powerful and all-knowing God, there is no such thing as an accident. Our God is in control. You will discover how much power you have in your life because of Him because you've taken the time to know Him.

KNOW GOD, SO HE KNOWS YOU

Those who take intentional time to know Him deeply are the ones Jesus and heaven know. The day will come when some who think they are Christians will say, "Lord, Lord, in Your name, we performed miracles, prophesied, and did many things for you." But Jesus will tell them, "I don't know you. Depart!" In reality, Jesus knows it all, but when He says, "I don't know you," he is saying that they operated under strange fire—unauthorized fire or anointing. These people never took the time to truly get to know the will of God and who He is. They were Martha's and did not choose the best part - to get to know Jesus as Mary did. If you don't take time to know who is this God you serve, He won't recognize you as an intimate worshiper.

This is a very scary thing. It makes me tremble just to think of it. We cannot be deep worshipers, let alone revival worshipers, if we operate under strange and unauthorized fire. It is one thing to sing about God, and a completely different thing to minister to God with our singing and to worship knowing whom you are worshiping.

When we do this, it takes a whole different meaning, approach, and level of engagement. This creates an automatic connection to the tones of the throne that bring a spirit of freedom to all. We become one with the Lord's Spirit, in one spirit with the Lord. The result is revival.

This revival comes in levels as remain engaged and faithful to God. Revival starts with you first. The deeper you get to know God and the more united with the Spirit you are, the higher you will be able to take people to levels of revival. You will become a conduit of His glory and power to bring revival not just to your church, family, and sphere of influence but also to your city, state, country, and the ends of the world. Some people think of a revival as an opportunity for them to become known, but those are diabolical motives since their only intention is personal glory.

When you get to know who God is, you will be able to open a whole world of possibilities no matter how old you are or what country you are from. As you intentionally seek to know who God is, you will open your mind to a paradigm shift. Your life will no longer be about just you. It will shift to be completely about Him and what matters most to Him.

This will turn you into a true revival worshiper of the King. It will create a bonding, synchronizing, and alignment where you realize life is more than you thought it was. It is no longer about you or me but about Him. Everything started with our Creator, and this earthly life will end with Him.

The enemy does not want us to know more about who God is because we would have a paradigm shift and be revived. But as you internalize these names of God to see who He is, you will know the truth, and the truth will set you free to be who God called you to be. Jesus Christ is the embodiment of truth; as a result, it is imperative that we deepen our understanding of the Truth—Himself. Enjoy your new journey as you intentionally start getting to know God's nature in a deeper, more intimate way!

Let's make God famous!

1,290 Names, Attributes, Truths, and Works to Know God

1. The I AM WHO I AM (Exodus 3:14)
2. Jesus, the I AM (John 8:58)
3. Lord God, You are One (John 10:30)
4. God, Name above all names throughout all times (Philippians 2:9)
5. Father, the great God who formed all things (Colossians 1:16)
6. God, You were before the day was (Psalm 90:2)
7. God, You are all Your names (Proverbs 18:10)
8. The God above all (John 3:31; Psalm 97:9)
9. God, the King of heaven (Daniel 4:34–37)
10. The God who is feared by the kings of the earth (Psalm 76:12)
11. The God who removes kings and sets up other kings (Daniel 2:21)
12. The supreme King seated on a great white throne (Revelation 20:11–15)
13. The Lord and King of the 24 elders and four living creatures (Revelation 19:4)

14. The loving King in the inner chamber (Song of Solomon 1:4)
15. The King who enchants me with the fragrance of His love (Song of Solomon 1:3)
16. Jesus, the Rabbi, Son of God, the King of Israel (John 1:49; Matthew 27:11)
17. Jesus, King of the Jews (Matthew 27:37; John 19:21)
18. Jesus, the King of Zion (Matthew 21:5)
19. Jesus, the Prince and Ruler of the kings of the earth (Revelation 1:5)
20. Jesus Christ, the eternal King of the nations forever and ever (Psalm 10:6; 1 Timothy 1:17)
21. God, the great King of all kingdoms (2 Kings 19:15; Psalm 68:32)
22. Lord of the kingdom, You rule over the nations (Psalm 22:28
23. God, the most and highest Sovereign of the kings (1 Timothy 6:11-19)
24. God, the great King over of all ages (1 Timothy 1:17)
25. God, the King of all heaven and earth (Psalm 146:6; Daniel 4:37)
26. God, the King of the saints (Revelation 6)
27. God, the Lord and King of peace (Hebrews 7:2)
28. God, my invincible, one and only, great King (1 Timothy 1:17)
29. God, the King of kings (Revelation 19:16; 1 Timothy 6:15)
30. God, my everlasting King (Romans 16:23)
31. The Lord of kings (Daniel 2:47)
32. God, the King of glory (Psalm 24:8)
33. The Lord and King of the universe (Hebrews 11:3)

34. Jesus, the Ruler of all the kings of the world (Revelation 1:5)
35. God, Your rule is everlasting (Daniel 4:34–37)
36. God, the Most High and honored (Daniel 4:34–37)
37. Father, the great and dreadful God (Malachi 4:5)
38. My Father, God (Ephesians 4:6)
39. God, the righteous Father (John 17:25)
40. God, my heavenly and eternal Father (Isaiah 9:6)
41. God, the Father, the vine grower (John 15:1)
42. God, the wonderful Counselor, mighty God, everlasting Father, great Prince of peace (Isaiah 9:26)
43. God, Abba, Father (Mark 14:36)
44. Lord, You are the God and Father of all (Ephesians 4:6)
45. Jesus, the Head of every man (1 Corinthians 11:3)
46. God, the Father of glory (Ephesians 1:17)
47. God, the Father of our spirits who gives life forever (Hebrews 12:9)
48. God, the Father to the fatherless and orphans (Psalm 68:5)
49. God, the Defender of the widows (Psalm 68:5)
50. God, the Father of lights (James 1:17)
51. God, the Father of mercies (2 Corinthians 1:13)
52. God, the Father of my Lord, Jesus Christ (2 Corinthians 11:31)
53. The Father who did not spare His own Son (Romans 8:32)
54. God, my everlasting Father (Isaiah 9:6)
55. Jesus, the great I AM (Revelation 1:8)
56. Jesus, appointed as judge of the living and the dead (1 Peter 4:4)

57. God, the Judge of judges (Genesis 18:25; 20:11-15; Psalms 94:2; 82:1; Job 12:17)
58. God, the righteous Judge of all creation (Psalm 67:4; Revelation 19:11)
59. God, the Justifier of those who have faith in Jesus (Romans 3:26)
60. God, the One who loves justice (Psalm 11:7; Psalm 82:2)
61. God, the impartial and unbiased Judge, Your judgments are all fair (Romans 2:11; John 5:22; Deuteronomy 10:17)
62. God, the Lord over kings (Daniel 2:47)
63. God, the revealer of mysteries (Daniel 2:47)
64. Jesus, the way (John 14:6)
65. Jesus, the truth (John 14:6)
66. Jesus, the Your name is alive (Revelation 1:18; Luke 24:23)
67. Jesus, the Word of God (John 1:1)
68. Jesus, the VERB (John 1:1)
69. Jesus, the Word of life (John 1:4)
70. Jesus, the child in the manger (Luke 2:12)
71. Jesus, the most powerful name like none other (Acts 4:12; John 17:11)
72. Jesus, the chief cornerstone (1 Peter 2:6)
73. Jesus, the minister of the sanctuary (Hebrews 8:2)
74. Jesus, the minister of the true tabernacle (Hebrews 8:2)
75. Jesus, a man of sorrows and acquainted with grief (Isaiah 53:3)
76. Jesus, a light to enlighten the gentiles (Luke 2:32)
77. Jesus, the great high priest (Hebrews 4:14)
78. Jesus, my secure place (Psalm 46:1)

79. Jesus, the author of our faith (Hebrews 12:2)
80. Jesus, my place of broad rivers and streams (Isaiah 33:21)
81. Jesus, a plant of renown (Ezekiel 34:29)
82. Jesus, clothed with majesty (Zechariah 6:13)
83. Jesus, a priest upon His throne (Zechariah 6:13)
84. Jesus, my Prince and my Savior (1 Timothy 2:3)
85. Christ Jesus, my Lord (1 Timothy 1:12)
86. Lord God, who lives from eternity to eternity (1 Chronicles 16:36)
87. Jesus, the Savior of the world (Matthew 1:21)
88. Jesus, my personal Savior (Romans 10:9-10)
89. Lord, outside of You, there is no Savior (Isaiah 43:11)
90. Jesus, sitting at the right hand of the Father (Mark 16:19)
91. Jesus, the great Gift (Romans 5:15)
92. Jesus, You are the life; no one comes to the Father except through You (John 14:6)
93. Jesus, the good news of great joy (Luke 2:10)
94. Jesus, the One who ascended to the Father (John 20:17)
95. God, the eternal, immortal, invisible one (1 Timothy 1:17)
96. The God who struck down mighty kings (Psalm 136:17)
97. God, You are righteous (Psalm 119:137)
98. The Most High, worthy of being feared, great King over all the earth (Psalm 47:2)
99. The great King and Lord of hosts—His name is feared among the nations (Malachi 1:14)
100. Jesus Christ, the Messiah (John 4:26)

101. Jesus Christ, my Lord (John 13:13)
102. The Lord who shows mercy from generation to generation to all who fear You (Luke 1:50)
103. Jesus, my rock of offense (1 Peter 2:8)
104. Jesus, a rod out of the stem of Jesse (Isaiah 11:1)
105. Jesus, the star out of Jacob (Numbers 24:17)
106. Jesus, the beginning of the creation of God (Revelation 3:14)
107. Jesus, the apostle and high priest of my profession (Hebrews 3:1)
108. Jesus, the author and finisher of my faith (Hebrews 12:2)
109. Jesus, the author of eternal salvation (Hebrews 5:9)
110. Jesus, the advocate who pleads my case before the Father (1 John 2:1)
111. Jesus, a stone in Zion, a tested stone (Isaiah 28:16)
112. Jesus, my Passover (1 Corinthians 5:7)
113. Jesus, the Head of the Church (Ephesians 5:23; Colossians 1:18)
114. Jesus Christ, You are supreme over all who rise from the dead (Colossians 1:18)
115. Jesus, You are first in everything (Colossians 1:18)
116. Jesus, who raised a kingdom of priests for God Your Father (Revelation 1:6)
117. Jesus, a precious cornerstone for a sure foundation (Isaiah 28:16-17)
118. Jesus, the Captain of our salvation (Hebrews 2:10-11)
119. Jesus, the covenant of the people (Hebrews 8:6)
120. Jesus, my dayspring from on high (Luke 1:78)
121. Jesus, the desire of all nations (Haggai 2:7)
122. Jesus, the first-begotten of the dead (Revelation 1:5)
123. The God, Agape Love (John 3:16; Romans 3:5)

124. Jesus, the firstborn of every creature (Colossians 1:15)
125. The God who killed the firstborn of Egypt (Psalms 135:8; 136:10)
126. Jesus, You are a priest forever in the order of Melchizedek (Hebrews 7:17)
127. Jesus, God's anointed one (2 Corinthians 1:21)
128. Jesus, the Heir of all things (Hebrews 1:2)
129. Jesus, the Head of the body (Colossians 1:18)
130. God, the rose of Sharon (Song of Solomon 2:1)
131. God, You are the lily of the valleys (Songs of Solomon 2:1)
132. Jesus, the God who has built His house, the Church (Matthew 7:24–27)
133. Jesus, the light, luminous, glowing, and radiant One (Psalm 76:4)
134. Jesus, the God who baptized me with His Holy Spirit and fire (Matthew 3:11)
135. Jesus, the God who washed me from my sins (Psalm 51:2)
136. Jesus, the God who shall come soon (Revelation 22:12)
137. Jesus, the God with world dominion (Psalm 22:28)
138. Jesus, the Chosen of God (Luke 23:35)
139. Jesus, the God who holds the key of David (Revelation 3:7)
140. Jesus, the God who comes from above (John 3:31)
141. Jesus, the righteous servant, and leader (Acts 24:7)
142. The Lord Jesus, the one who comes in the name of the Lord (Matthew 21:9)
143. Jesus, the beloved Son of God most high (Mark 3:17)
144. God, Jesus Christ the righteous (1 John 2:1)

145. God, Jesus of Nazareth (Matthew 26:71)
146. Jesus, the radiance of God's glory (Hebrews 1:3)
147. Jesus, the exact representation of God's nature (Hebrews 1:3)
148. Jesus, who upholds all things by the word of His power (Hebrews 1:3)
149. Jesus, You are much better than the angels, with a more excellent name than they (Hebrews 1:4)
150. Jesus, who delivered us from the wrath to come (1 Thessalonians 1:10)
151. Jesus, the image of the invisible God (Colossians 1:15)
152. Jesus, the firstborn of every creature (Colossians 1:15)
153. Jesus, the appointed heir of all things (Hebrews 1:2)
154. The God of the spotted and speckled (Genesis 30:39)
155. Jesus, the forerunner (Hebrews 6:20)
156. Jesus, crowned with glory and honor (Hebrews 2:9)
157. Jesus, the mediator of a new and better covenant (Hebrews 8:6)
158. Jesus, the mediator of the New Testament (Hebrews 9:15; 12:24)
159. Jesus, the Lion of the tribe of Judah (Revelation 5:5)
160. God, Jesus of Nazareth (John 18:5)
161. Holy Spirit, the unspeakable gift (2 Corinthians 9:15)
162. Jesus, the Prince of life (Acts 3:15)
163. Jesus, the Rabboni (John 20:16)
164. Jesus, the Prince of peace, prophesied by Isaiah (Isaiah 9:26)

165. Jesus, the Prince of princes (Daniel 8:25)
166. Jesus, the Son of David (Matthew 9:27)
167. Jesus, the Son of man (Matthew 24:30)
168. Jesus, the Son of the Blessed (Mark 14:61)
169. Jesus, the Son of the Father (2 John 1:3)
170. Jesus, the Son of the Highest (Mark 14:62)
171. Jesus, the Son of the living God (Matthew 26:63)
172. Jesus, the root of David (Revelation 5:5)
173. Jesus, the root of Jesse (Isaiah 11.1)
174. Jesus, the seed of Abraham (John 8:33)
175. God, the Shepherd, and Bishop of my soul (1 Peter 2:25)
176. Jesus, the righteous Branch (Jeremiah 33:15)
177. Jesus, the Prophet (John 4:19)
178. Jesus, the Promised One (Isaiah 25:8-9)
179. Jesus, the last Adam (Romans 5:14)
180. Jesus, the light of the world (John 8:12)
181. Jesus, the living bread which came down from heaven (John 6:51–59)
182. Jesus, the Holy One of God (John 6:69)
183. Jesus, the brightness of God's glory (Hebrews 1:3)
184. Jesus, the chief cornerstone (1 Peter 2:6)
185. Jesus, the Author of eternal life
186. Jesus, the incarnate truth (1 John 5:6)
187. God, the giver of eternal life (John 10:28)
188. Jesus, the sun of righteousness (Malachi 4:2)
189. The God who speaks in righteousness (Isaiah 63:1)
190. The Lord whose eyes are on the righteous (Psalm 34:15)
191. The Lord whose ears are attentive to my cry (Psalm 34:15)
192. The God who restores my soul (Psalm 23)

193. The God who guides me in the paths of righteousness (Psalm 23)
194. The God who is mighty to save (Isaiah 63:1)
195. The One who is majestic in His apparel (Isaiah 63:1)
196. The One who marches in the greatness of His strength (Isaiah 63:1)
197. Jesus, the atoning sacrifice for my sins (1 John 2:2)
198. Jesus, the resurrection, and the life (John 11:25)
199. Jesus, the stone which the builders rejected (1 Peter 2:7)
200. Jesus, the true bread from heaven (John 6:32)
201. God, the Spirit of adoption (Romans 8:15)
202. God, the Spirit of Christ (1 Peter 1:11)
203. God, the Holy Spirit, and my intercessor (Romans 8:34)
204. God, Your Holy Spirit is the context of Your Word (John 16:12–15)
205. God, the Holy Spirit, a witness to us (Hebrews 10:15)
206. God, the Holy Spirit, my counselor (John 14:26)
207. Holy Spirit, the promise of the Father (Luke 24:49)
208. Holy Spirit, the comforter (John 14:26)
209. Holy Spirit, the earnest of my inheritance (Ephesians 1:14)
210. God, the Divine Trinity, three in one (1 John 5:7)
211. God, the Father, Son, and Holy Spirit (Matthew 28:19)
212. God, You are Deity (Colossians 2:9)
213. The One and Only God (1 Corinthians 8:6)
214. The Sovereign God (Psalm 135:6)
215. The Lord will reign forever (Psalm 146:12)

216. The God of wonders, signs, and mighty miracles (Hebrews 2:4; Psalm 13:4)
217. The God who works wonders (Psalm 77:14)
218. You are the Lord, the God of all mankind; nothing is hard for you (Jeremiah 32:27)
219. The God who made wonderful works to be remembered (Psalm 111:4)
220. God, the origin of everything (Genesis 1:1)
221. God, the immutable (Malachi 3:6; 1 Peter 1:25)
222. God, the great, infallible teacher (John 3:2)
223. The God of generosity (Psalms 145:6;19)
224. The God of honor and reverence (1 Samuel 2:30; Exodus 3:5)
225. The Father who honors me (John 12:26)
226. The God of all-sufficiency who makes me sufficient (2 Corinthians 3:5)
227. The God of favor (Psalms 5:12)
228. The God of peace (Romans 15:3)
229. God, You are love (1 John 4:8)
230. Jesus, the Sower and Lord of the harvest (Luke 10:2)
231. The God who loved the world sacrificially, giving His only Son (John 3:16)
232. God, the Author and Creator of love (1 John 4:19; 1 John 4:8)
233. The God who loves me unconditionally (Romans 5:8; Ephesians 2:8)
234. God, Your unfailing love is better than life itself (Psalm 63:3)
235. God, Your love is deeper than the ocean; it has no limits (Psalm 36:5–7)
236. The God of patience (Exodus 34:6)

237. The God who is full of new mercies every morning (Lamentations 3:23)
238. The Lord, full of compassion and mercy (James 5:11)
239. God, the one who weeps with those who weep (Romans 12:15)
240. God, who keeps covenant and mercy forever (Psalm 105:8; Deuteronomy 7:9)
241. The God of my heart's mercy (Psalm 51)
242. The God of mercy (Ephesians 2:4–5)
243. The God of the rich and the poor (Proverbs 22:2)
244. God, the all-knowing one (John 18:4)
245. God, the shelter and refuge of the poor (Psalm 9:9)
246. God, the all-seeing (Genesis 16:13)
247. God, You will hold me up wherever I go (Psalm 91)
248. God, the refuge of salvation for Your anointed ones (Psalm 28:8)
249. God, my rock, my tower of refuge (Psalm 18:2)
250. God, my refuge and strength from the storm (Psalm 46:1)
251. The God of the stranger (Psalm 146:9)
252. God, the author and founder of marriage between one man and one woman (Genesis 2:18, 22–24; Matthew 19:8)
253. The God who heals the brokenhearted (Psalm 147:3)
254. The God who is close to the brokenhearted (Psalm 34:18)
255. The God of promise (Hebrews 6:13)
256. The God of covenants (Genesis 2:4)
257. The God of the feasts (Deuteronomy 16:15; Nehemiah 10:33)

258. The God of happiness (Matthew 25:21; Psalm 146:5)
259. The God of contentment (Song of Solomon 8:10)
260. The God surrounded by light (Daniel 2:22)
261. The God who is, who was, and who is to come, the Almighty (Revelation 1:8)
262. The God of the sevenfold Spirit of God and the seven stars (Revelation 3:1)
263. The God of the kingdom of priests (Revelation 1:6)
264. God, the faithful one forever (2 Chronicles 5:13)
265. God, the true and faithful witness of all things (Revelation 1:5; Jeremiah 42:5)
266. Jesus called faithful and true (Revelation 19:11)
267. God, Your faithful promises are my armor and protection (Psalm 91:4)
268. Jesus, the merciful and faithful high priest (Hebrews 2:17)
269. The Lord with a powerful and majestic voice (Psalm 29:4)
270. The God of lightning and thunders (Exodus 19:16; Psalm 29:3-4; Psalm 18:13)
271. The God of glory thunder (Psalm 29:3)
272. The God who thunders over the mighty sea (Psalm 29:3)
273. The Lord whose voice thunders like the mighty ocean. (Revelation 4:5; Job 40:9)
274. God, the divine Inventor, and Creator of innovation (Revelation 21:5; Exodus 31:2–11)
275. God, the creative one (Ephesians 3:9)
276. God, the Creator of the earth (Genesis 1:1)
277. The God of the Psalms (Psalms)
278. The God that made me lie down in green pastures (Psalm 23)

279. The God who leads me beside quiet waters (Psalm 23)
280. God, the Creator, and designer of humankind (Genesis 1:26–2:25)
281. The Creator and designer of all babies (Jeremiah 1:5; Psalm 139:13–24)
282. God, the Creator of all true worship (Revelation 4, 5:9–14)
283. God, the composer of songs of love (Zephaniah 3:17; Song of Songs)
284. God, the Author and Creator of sounds and rhythms (Psalm 150:3–6)
285. The Creator and Designer of the Tabernacle of David (Acts 15:16–17)
286. God, the all-self-sufficient, self-sustained, and self-created (Exodus 3:14; John 5:26; Acts 17:24)
287. God, the Creator of heaven (Genesis 14:19)
288. God, the Inventor, and Creator of the great lights (Genesis 1:16)
289. God, You are mightier than the thunders of the many waters (Psalm 93:4)
290. God, the faithful Creator (1 Peter 4:19)
291. God, Creator of all angelic beings and spirits (Revelation 5:11)
292. The Divine Designer of nature (Romans 1:20)
293. The God of marvelous glory and excellence (2 Peter 1:3)
294. God, the author of the genders of man and woman (Genesis 2:4–25)
295. God, whose Spirit moves on the surface of the sea (Genesis 1:2)
296. God, the Mighty of the mighty (Jeremiah 9:3; Psalm 93:4)

297. The Lord who made the earth with great power and with outstretched arm (Jeremiah 32:17)
298. The God who blesses the humble (Matthew 5:5–15)
299. The Lord who blesses His people with peace (Psalm 29:11)
300. The God of the impossible, nothing is too difficult for You (Luke 18:27)
301. God, the Spirit of wisdom and understanding (Exodus 31:3; Isaiah 11:2; Colossians 1:9)
302. God, the Spirit of worship (John 4:23–24; Psalm 99)
303. God, the Spirit of prophecy (Revelation 19:10)
304. God, the incomparable (Colossians 1:13–20)
305. The God who makes Yourself known through visions (Numbers 12:6)
306. The God of Dunamis power (Matthew 22:29; Acts 1:8)
307. God, the tower of salvation (2 Samuel 22:51)
308. God, my superpower (Acts 1:8; 2 Chronicles 20:6; Psalm 71:18)
309. The God of the universe (Psalm 8:3-4)
310. God, You are my beauty, shine, and splendor (Psalm 50:2)
311. God, the giver of all revelation (Revelation 1:1)
312. God, Your splendor covers the heavens, and the earth is full of Your praise (Habakkuk 3:3)
313. God, the one who resurrects the dead (John 11:25)
314. Jesus Christ, the one who died and rose again (2 Corinthians 5:15)
315. Jesus, the one who died for my sins (Romans 5:8)
316. God, the one who does signs and wonders (Deuteronomy 6:22)

317. The God who searches the mind and the heart of humans (Jeremiah 17:10)
318. God, great and worthy of being greatly adored (Psalm 96:4)
319. You are Yahweh, a God compassionate and gracious (Exodus 34:6)
320. The Lord, slow to anger, overflowing with loyal love and faithfulness (Exodus 34:6–7)
321. God, the defender of Your people Israel (Isaiah 49:7)
322. Jesus, the Savior of Israel (Acts 13:23)
323. Jesus, the consolation of Israel (Luke 2:25)
324. God, the Father of Israel (Jeremiah 31:9)
325. God, the Mighty One of Israel (Isaiah 1:24)
326. The God of the armies of Israel (1 Samuel 17:45)
327. Jehovah, the God of the twelve tribes of Israel (Acts 7:8)
328. The God of the Hebrews (Exodus 5:3; 7:16)
329. God, the great governor of the world (Isaiah 33:22)
330. God, the great guide of my life (Isaiah 33:22)
331. Holy Spirit, the one who revives the soul (Psalm 19:7)
332. The Lord, my Agnus Dei (John 1:29)
333. God, my best friend (John 15:15)
334. God, my lawgiver (Psalm 119:138)
335. The Lord who cares for those who trust in You (1 Peter 5:7; Nahum 1:7)
336. The Lord, my redeemer (Isaiah 59:20; 54:5)
337. God, my healer (Acts 9:34)
338. God, my restorer (Isaiah 58:12; Acts 3:21)
339. God, my supreme worship (Romans 12:1–2; Deuteronomy 10:17)

340. The Lord who is supreme over all gods and over all powers (Deuteronomy 10:17)
341. God, my new love song (Psalms 89:1; 98:1)
342. The Lord, the song of my heart (Psalm 40:3; Ephesians 5:19)
343. Jesus, You are the true grapevine (John 15:1–8)
344. God, You made me for You (Psalm 100:3; Isaiah 43:21)
345. God, You created me for Your glory (Isaiah 43:7)
346. God, You created me to worship You eternally (1 Peter 2:9; Isaiah 43:7)
347. The God who speaks and silences the whole earth (Habakkuk 2:20)
348. The God who declares new things before they happen (Isaiah 42:9)
349. The God who has the answer for everything (Jeremiah 33:3; Daniel 10:12; Luke 1:37)
350. God, the source of living waters (Jeremiah 2:13)
351. God, the source of the water of life who gives freely to all who are thirsty (Revelation 21:6)
352. God, the giver of dreams and visions (Numbers 12:6; Daniel 1:17)
353. The Lord, my God (Exodus 6: 7)
354. The Lord, and apart from You there is no God (Isaiah 44:6)
355. The God who wounds and heals (Deuteronomy 32:39)
356. The God who kills and gives life (Deuteronomy 32:39)
357. God, no one can be rescued from your powerful hand (Deuteronomy 32:39)
358. God, there is no other god but You (Deuteronomy 32:39)

359. God, You are my owner (Jeremiah 3:14)
360. God, You are my rest (Psalm 62:1)
361. The Almighty God who wants me to walk before You and be perfect (Genesis 17:1)
362. God, who establishes His covenant with me and will multiply me greatly (Genesis 17:2)
363. The God who redeems us (Titus 2:14)
364. The God who rescued me from the domain of darkness (Colossians 1:13)
365. The God who transferred me to the kingdom of His beloved Son (Colossians 1:13)
366. The God who calls me to fear nothing (Isaiah 41:10; Psalm 27:1)
367. The God who has called me by name and says, "You are mine." (Isaiah 43:1; 49:1)
368. God, my helper, and sustainer (Psalm 54:4)
369. Lord, the God of my life (Psalms 146:2; 27:1)
370. Lord, you are my life eternally (Psalm 42:8)
371. God, the one who empowers us to make riches (Deuteronomy 8:18)
372. The Lord, the God of all flesh (Jeremiah 32:27)
373. The Lord, my inheritance and possession (Ezekiel 44:28)
374. God, You give favor to those whom You choose (Exodus 33:18)
375. The God who favors Zion with His goodness (Psalm 51:18)
376. The God of the poor and the rich (1 Samuel 2:7)
377. The God who justifies me (Romans 5:1; Galatians 2:16)
378. The God who restores my soul and guides me along paths of justice for the love of His name (Psalm 23:3)

379. Jesus, the friend of sinners (Matthew 11:19; Luke 7:34)
380. The God who never lies and never will (Numbers 23:19; Hebrews 6:18)
381. The God who cries with those who cry (Romans 12:15; John 11:35)
382. The God who answers my cry (Psalm 34:17; Jeremiah 33:3)
383. The God of meekness, patient and humble of heart (Colossians 3:12; Ephesians 4:2)
384. The God who is spirit (John 4:24)
385. The God who erases my transgressions for love of Yourself and will not remember my sins (Isaiah 43:25)
386. The God who forgives my iniquity and transgression (Numbers 14:18)
387. God, the manna who descended from heaven (John 3:13)
388. God, You are all the colors of the rainbows (Ezekiel 1:26–28)
389. The God who will not remember my sins (Hebrews 8:12)
390. God, the forgiver of all iniquity past, present, and future (1 John 1:9)
391. The Lord God, a victorious warrior (Zephaniah 3:17)
392. The Lord God who is in our midst (Zephaniah 3:17)
393. The Lord who quietly calms me in His love (Zephaniah 3:17)
394. God, the beloved in Songs of Songs (Song of Songs 6:3; Revelation 19:7)

395. The God who extends Your hands to me (Psalm 90:17)
396. God, my deliverer (Psalm 32:7; Colossians 1:13; Micah 2:13)
397. God, the altar of peace for my fears (Judges 6:24)
398. The God who makes the simple wise (Psalm 19:7)
399. God, the one who comforts me (Isaiah 51:12)
400. God the Lord, Yeshua, the God of compassion and loving-kindness (Psalm 25:6)
401. The Lord my God, and there is no other like You (Joel 2:27)
402. God, the living bread that came down from heaven; if anyone eats this bread, he will live forever (John 6:51)
403. The God from above; You are not of this world (John 8:23)
404. Jesus, You are the door for salvation (John 10:9)
405. God, the good shepherd who lays down His life for the sheep (John 10:11)
406. God, the shepherd who knows Your sheep, and they know You (John10:14)
407. The Lord, my Shepherd, I shall not want (Psalm 23:1)
408. Jesus, You are the way (John 14:6)
409. Jesus, the absolute truth (John 14:6)
410. Jesus, the root and offspring of David, the bright morning star (Revelation 22:16)
411. The God of my salvation (Psalms 35:3; 25:5)
412. The God who supplies the food in my house (Genesis1:29)
413. The Lord who took me out of a life without direction to give me a land to possess (Genesis 15:7)

414. The God of justice (Psalm 50:6; 1 Chronicles 16:14)
415. The God who gives justice to the oppressed (Psalms 146:7; 82:3)
416. The God who gives food to the hungry (Psalm 146:7)
417. God, the Lord of lords (1 Timothy 6:15; Psalm 136:3)
418. The Lord my God, Your name is Jealous (Exodus 34:14; Deuteronomy 5:9)
419. God, who jealously desires the Spirit He has made to dwell in us (James 4:5)
420. The God who gives greater grace (James 4:6)
421. The God who gives grace to the humble (James 4:6)
422. The God who will not hold the culprit innocent (Numbers 14:18)
423. The God who gives the wild donkey its freedom (Job 39:5)
424. God, by Your understanding, the hawk soars and stretches his wings toward the south (Job 39:26)
425. God, by Your command, the eagle mounts up and makes his nest on high (Job 39:27)
426. The God who gives the horse his might and clothes his neck with a mane (Job 39:19)
427. God, You are with the generation of the righteous (Psalm 14:5)
428. Jesus, the righteous one (1 John 2:1)
429. The God whose precepts are right and make the heart rejoice (Psalm 19:8)
430. The Lord whose commandment is pure and enlightens the eyes (Psalm 19:8)

431. God, the one who makes unbreakable covenants and pacts with humans (Genesis 17:7)
432. God, the holy, pure, immaculate one (1 Peter 1:16)
433. God, before You no other god was formed, nor will there be after You (Isaiah 43:10)
434. The God who weighs all actions (1 Samuel 2:3)
435. God, all Your words are true and correct (Psalm 119:160)
436. God, the one who never makes a mistake (Genesis 18)
437. The God who keeps all His promises (Psalm 145:13)
438. God, Your commandments illuminate my eyes (Psalm 19:8)
439. God, your holy commandments bring freedom (Psalm 119:45)
440. God, You are a witness in my favor (John 5:32)
441. Lord, You are in Your holy temple (Psalm 138:2)
442. God, You rule from heaven (Daniel 4:26)
443. God, who watches over everyone closely (1 Peter 3:12)
444. God, who examines both the righteous and the wicked (Psalm 11:4)
445. The God who hates those who love violence (Psalm 11:4)
446. The Lord, Creator of everything and made all things (Colossians 1:16)
447. God, You alone stretched out the heavens (Isaiah 44:24)
448. Lord, the heavens proclaim Your glory (Psalm 19:1)
449. Lord, the expanse of the heavens announces the work of your hands (Psalm 19:1)

450. The God who builds His lofty palace in the heavens (Amos 9:6)
451. The God who sits in the heavens and upon the circle of the earth (Isaiah 40:22)
452. God, the one who sits on heaven's mercy seat (Hebrews 9:5–12; Romans 3:25)
453. God, the majesty in the heavens (Psalms 29:4; 93:1)
454. Lord, Your voice is powerful and full of majesty (Psalm 29:4)
455. The Lord who made the heavens skillfully by His wisdom (Psalm 136:5)
456. The Lord who made the heavens by His word (Psalm 33:6)
457. The Lord who made His army by the breath of His mouth (Psalm 33:6)
458. The God of ordinance (Psalm 81:4)
459. The God of the law (Psalm 119:138; Matthew 5:17–18)
460. The God of His statutes, to walk in them (1 King 2:3)
461. The God who is to be feared, and we tremble in Your presence (Psalm 115:13; Deuteronomy 6:24; Jeremiah 5:22)
462. The God who placed the sand as a boundary for the sea and made it an eternal decree (Jeremiah 5:22)
463. The God of total forgiveness (Romans 3:23; Psalm 130:3–4)
464. God, the most essential One (Matthew 6:33; Colossians 3:10)
465. Christ, You are all in all (Colossians 3:11)

466. The God who loves the godly (Psalm 146:8)
467. The God who protects the foreigners (Psalm 146:9)
468. The God who cares for the orphans and widows (Psalm 146:9)
469. Jesus, appointed heir and lawful owner of all things (Hebrews 1:2)
470. God, the Lord before whom every knee shall bow, and every tongue shall confess (Romans 14:11)
471. God, nobody can revoke Your deeds (Romans 11:29; Galatians 3:17)
472. The God who refines, molds, and forms you (Zechariah 13:9)
473. The God who calls me His, and calls me by His name (Isaiah 43:1)
474. Lord, You search the hearts and examine secret motives (Jeremiah 17:10)
475. The Lord who gives all people their due rewards according to what their actions deserve (Revelation 22:12; Jeremiah 17:10; Hebrews 11:6)
476. God, vengeance is Yours, the avenger (Hebrews 10:30)
477. God, the Prince of the shepherds (1 Peter 5:4)
478. God, the shepherd's rod (Psalm 23:4)
479. God, you are my great pastor; I will lack nothing (Psalm 23)
480. The God whose throne is in Heaven (Psalm 11:4; Isaiah 66:1)
481. God, You are the rod that protects me and brings comfort (Psalm 23:4)
482. God, You are tender with me in the desert (Hosea 2:14)
483. God, the one who can be trusted (1 Corinthians 1:9–11)

484. The God who makes my way perfect (Psalm 18:32)
485. The God who makes me as surefooted as a deer (Psalm 18:32–33)
486. The God who enables me to stand on mountain heights (Psalm 18:32–33)
487. God, the Creator, and owner of silver and gold (Haggai 2:8–10)
488. God, my protector (Psalm 18:2)
489. God, my provider (Matthew 6:25–34)
490. God, those united with You are one with you (1 Corinthians 6:17)
491. God, the Spirit of counsel and might (Isaiah 11:2–3)
492. God, full of tenderness and affection (Philippians 1:8)
493. The God who frees me from all fear and doubt (Isaiah 41:10)
494. God, You are a friend, closer than a brother (Proverbs 18:24)
495. The God who is with me in the valley of the shadow of death (Psalm 23)
496. The God who is always with me and never abandons me (Psalm 94:14; John 8:29)
497. God, the lamp who lights my way (Psalm 119:105)
498. God, Your government, and its peace will never end (Isaiah 9:7)
499. God, the way of holiness (Isaiah 35:8)
500. Lord, You are surrounded with honor and majesty (Psalm 96:6)
501. Lord, Your strength and beauty fill Your sanctuary (Psalm 96:6)
502. The God of peace who calms me in the storms (Matthew 8:23)

503. The God of rest for the weary and those burdened (Matthew 11:28-30)
504. The God who wipes away all my tears (Revelation 21:4)
505. The God who delivers the righteous from all their afflictions (Psalm 34:19)
506. Jesus, the Great Physician (Jeremiah 8:22)
507. The Lord who sanctifies me (Leviticus 22:32)
508. The Lord, the one who formed me from the womb (Jeremiah 1:5; Isaiah 49:5)
509. God, the magnified one (Philippians 1:10; Daniel 11:37)
510. The God of rewards (Hebrews 11:6; Colossians 3:23–24)
511. The God of my great reward (Genesis 15:1; Genesis 17:8)
512. Lord, You are so good to all, all the time (Psalms 34:8; 135:3; 145:9; 2 Chronicles 5:13)
513. Lord, Your unfailing love continues forever (Psalm 117:2)
514. Lord, Your faithfulness continues to all generations (Psalm 100:5)
515. Lord, Your faithful love endures forever (Psalm 136:1)
516. God, the great giver (John 3:16; Ephesians 2:8–9)
517. The God who never sleeps (Psalm 121:4)
518. God, the preparer of my place in heaven (John 14:3)
519. The God who gives me much more than all I can ask or think (Ephesians 3:20)
520. God, the source of all true wealth (Proverbs 10:22; Deuteronomy 8:17–18)

521. God, the Spirit of freedom who frees me (2 Corinthians 3:17; Romans 8:2)
522. God, the One who gives me joy and peace in the trials (Psalms 94:19; 30:5)
523. The God who anoints my head with oil (Psalm 23:5)
524. Jesus, the bridegroom who will return for His bride, the church (Matthew 9:15)
525. The Lord who looks at those who tremble at His word (Isaiah 66:5)
526. Lord, even the demons believe and tremble with fear before You (James 2:19)
527. The God who prepares a table for me in the presence of my enemies (Psalm 23:2–5)
528. The God who anointed my head with oil and made my cup overflow (Psalm 23:2–5)
529. The Lord who is among any two or three who gather in His name (Matthew 18:20)
530. The God who hears all my prayers and answers them (John 5:14)
531. The God of the brave and courageous (2 Samuel 10:12)
532. God, the one who calms my fears (Psalm 34:4)
533. God, the one who prospers me (Psalm 106:5)
534. God, the righteous reward of all who seek You (Hebrews 11:6)
535. God, the giver of all abundant life (John 10:10)
536. God, You are higher and greater than I can feel, think, or see (1 Corinthians 2:9; Isaiah 55:8–9)
537. God, the source of all life (Psalms 68:26; 87:7)
538. God, the Lord who tests me to see if I walk in His law or not (Exodus 16:4)

539. God, the great warrior (Jeremiah 20:11)
540. God, the banner of war (Isaiah 59:19; Psalms 20:5; 60:4)
541. God, the two-edged sword (Hebrews 4:12)
542. God, my battle cry (Isaiah 42:13; Ephesians 6:10)
543. God, the victor—You always win, You never lose a battle (2 Chronicles 20:15; John 16:33)
544. God, my security and assurance in everything (Hebrews 11:1; Romans 5:5; Psalm 23:4
545. The God who annihilated Satan's plans (Hebrews 2:14)
546. God, the Spirit of power (Matthew 1:18; Micah 3:8)
547. God, the master planner of all nations and kingdoms (Isaiah 14:26; Jeremiah 10:7)
548. God, the great conqueror of death, hell, and the grave (Revelation 1:18)
549. Jesus, the one who holds the keys of death and the grave (Revelation 1:18)
550. Jesus, the living one who lives forevermore (Revelation 1:18)
551. God, You have possession of me (1 Peter 2:9)
552. God, Yours is the kingdom, the power, and the glory (1 Chronicles 29:11; Psalm 62:11)
553. The God who cast out the nations before me (Deuteronomy 9:4)
554. God, the great commander of the armies of heaven (Psalm 24:10)
555. Lord, You are a great and awesome God (Daniel 9:4)
556. The Lord Jehovah of the armies (Zechariah 1:3)
557. God, the defender of those who believes in You (Psalm 68:5)

558. The God who holds the sun, moon, and stars in their place (Psalm 8:3)
559. God, the mighty shield around me, my glory (Psalm 3:3)
560. God, the buckler, and shield to all those that trust in You (2 Samuel 22:31)
561. God, the one who holds my head high (Psalm 3:3)
562. God, the fullness of greatness, power, glory, victory, and majesty (1 Chronicles 29:11)
563. God, the sword of the Spirit (Ephesians 6:17)
564. The God who fills me with great victories (Psalm 18:50)
565. The God of eternity (Ecclesiastes 3:11)
566. The God who is the same today, yesterday, and forever (Hebrews 13:8)
567. Lord, You shower compassion on all Your creation (Psalm 145:9
568. God, the Alpha and the Omega, the first and the last, the beginning and the end (Revelation 22:13)
569. God, the one who builds the faith of men (1 Corinthians 3:10; Joshua 1:9)
570. God, the author and governor of the day and night (Psalm 74:16)
571. God, the uncreated, self-existent God (Genesis 3:14)
572. God, the unseen one who never dies, You alone are God (1 Timothy 1:17)
573. The God whose eyes contemplate everything (Psalm 11:4)
574. The God who is the same with me every day (Malachi 3:6)
575. God, You are not of this world (John 17:16)

576. The God who knows all my works through eternity (Acts 15:18)
577. The Lord God, Omnipresent (Jeremiah 23:24)
578. The Lord God, Omnipotent (Revelation 4:8; 11:17)
579. The Lord God, Omniscient (Psalm 44:21; Psalm 147:5)
580. The God who can see the beginning and the end simultaneously (Isaiah 46:10)
581. The God who fulfills His words (Joshua 21:45; Lamentations 2:17)
582. The God who is all in everything. (Ephesians 4:6; 1 Corinthians 15:28)
583. Jesus, the verb in the beginning (John 1:1)
584. The Lord is glorious and strong (Psalm 96:7)
585. God, who will cause us to go in and out find pasture (John 10: 9)
586. God, the good master, and Lord (Matthew 23:8–10)
587. God, Immanuel—God with us (Isaiah 7:14, Isaiah 8:8–10, Matthew 1:23)
588. God, Jehovah-Shammah—The Lord is here (Ezekiel 48:35)
589. God, Adonai—The Lord; My great Lord God is the master and majestic Lord (Psalm 8; Isaiah 40:3–5; Ezekiel 16:8; Habakkuk 3:19)
590. God, Jehovah-Elohim—God is the all-powerful Creator of the universe (Genesis 1:1–3; Deuteronomy 10:17; Psalm 68, Mark 13:19)
591. God, El-Elyon—The Lord, Most High God and Exalted. (Genesis 14:17–22; Psalm 78:35; Daniel 4:34; Acts 16:17)

592. God, El Roí, —The God who sees me (Genesis 16:11–14; Psalm 139:7–12)
593. El Elohe Yisrael—God, the God of Israel (Genesis 33:20; Exodus 5:1; Psalm 68:8; Psalm 106:48)
594. Elohim Kedoshim—The Holy God (Joshua 24:19; Leviticus 19–20)
595. El Qanna—Lord, a jealous God (Exodus 20:5; Deuteronomy 5:9)
596. El Nekamoth—The avenger God (Psalm 18:47)
597. Elohim Ozer Li—God my helper (Psalm 54:4)
598. El Simchath Gili—The God of my exceeding joy (Psalm 43:4)
599. Elohim Chaseddi—God of my mercy (Psalm 59:10)
600. Lord, El Bethel—The God of the house of God (Gen 35:7–9)
601. El Hakabodh—The God of glory (Psalm 29:3)
602. God, Jehovah-Elohai—My God (Psalm 18:2)
603. Elohei Tehillati—The God of my praise (Psalm 109:1, 30)
604. Elohei Maozen—God of my strength (2 Samuel 22:33)
605. Elohei Marom—The God of heights (Micah 6:6)
606. Ehyeh Asher Ehyeh—The eternal all-sufficient God (Exodus 3:14)
607. Elohim Shophtim Ba-arets—The God who judges all the earth (Psalm 58:11)
608. Jehovah Chereb—The Lord, the Sword (Deuteronomy 33:29)
609. Jehovah El Gemuwal—The Lord God of recompense (Jeremiah 51:56)
610. Jehovah Elohim Yeshua—Jesus, the Son of God (Matthew 16:16)

611. You are Yeshua Ha Moshiach, Jesus our Messiah (Matthew 1:16)
612. Elohei Mikkarov—The God who is near (Jeremiah 23:23)
613. Sar-Shalom—God the Prince of peace (Isaiah 9:6)
614. Ruach Hakkodesh—God the Holy Spirit (Psalm 51:11)
615. Ruach Elohim—You are the great wind and Spirit of God (Genesis 1:2; 1 Samuel 10:10)
616. Jehovah Malakh—The angel of Jehovah (Genesis 12:7; Genesis 16:7–14)
617. Jehovah Magen—The Lord my shield (Genesis 15:1; Deuteronomy 33:29)
618. Or Goyim—Light of the nations (Isaiah 42:6)
619. Jehovah Tsemach—Jesus, the Branch of the Lord (Isaiah 4:2)
620. El-Shaddai—Almighty, omnipotent God (Genesis 17:1; Psalm 91:1)
621. God, El-Olam—The everlasting God (Isaiah 40:28; Psalm 90:2)
622. God, Yahweh—He who has life in Himself (Exodus 3:15)
623. God, Jehovah-Jireh—The Lord my provider (Genesis 22:13–14)
624. God, Jehovah-Nissi—The Lord my victorious banner (Exodus 17:15)
625. God, Jehovah-Shalom—The Lord my peace (Judges 6:24)
626. God, Jehovah-Sabot—Jehovah of armies (1 Samuel 1:3; Isaiah 6:1–3)
627. God, Jehovah-Mekaddishkem—You are the One who sanctifies me (Exodus 31:13)

628. God, Jehovah-Rohi—The Lord my shepherd/pastor (Psalm 23:1)
629. God, Jehovah-Shammah—The Lord who is present (Ezekiel 48:35)
630. God, Jehovah-Ropheka—The Lord my healer (Exodus 15:26)
631. God, Jehovah-Sabaoth, Elohim Tsebaoth-The Lord of Hosts (2 Samuel 5:10; Psalm 80:4, 7)
632. God, Jehovah-Tsidkenu—The Lord my righteousness (Jeremiah 23:6)
633. God, Jehovah-Hoseenu—The Lord my maker (Psalm 95)
634. God, Jehovah-Eloheenu—The Lord my God (Deuteronomy 1:6,19–20)
635. God, You are for me, in me, and over me (Acts 17:28; John 17:23)
636. The God of lovingkindness that endures forever (Psalm 136)
637. The God who makes all things new (Revelation 21:5; Isaiah 43:18–19)
638. The Holy God who is enthroned in the midst of His people's praises (Psalm 22:3)
639. The God who is married to His Church (Revelation 19:7–9)
640. God, the maker of all things (Jeremiah 51:19; Ecclesiastes 11:5)
641. The God of all flesh (Jeremiah 32:27)
642. The God who made everything beautiful in its own time (Ecclesiastes 3:11)
643. The God who divided the sea in two (Psalms 136:13)
644. The God who teaches me (Isaiah 48:17)

645. The God who sets me free (Romans 8:2, 6, 13)
646. The God who delivers me (Psalms 34:4; 40:13)
647. The God who intercedes for me always (Romans 8:26–27, 33–34)
648. The God who answers me in the day of anguish (Psalm 118:5)
649. The God who calls things that are not as if they were (Romans 4:17)
650. The God who comforts me in the day of tribulation (2 Corinthians 1:4)
651. The God who commanded that light shine out of darkness (2 Corinthians 4:6)
652. The God who made the light shine in my heart so I could know the glory of God (2 Corinthians 4:6)
653. The God who covers me with light like a cloak (Psalm 104:2)
654. The God who crowns me with an everlasting love and tender goodness (Psalm 103:4)
655. The God who carries me in His arms each day (Psalm 68:19)
656. The God who rescues me from death (Psalm 68:19)
657. The God who dwells on high (Isaiah 57:15; 33:5; Psalm 91)
658. The God who gave Himself as a ransom for everyone (1 Timothy 2:6)
659. The God who gives food to every living thing. (Psalm 136:25)
660. The God who sends the rain on the earth (Job 5:10; Zechariah 10:1)
661. The God who gives me all things abundantly for my enjoyment (1 Timothy 6:17)

662. The God who identified me as His own and has given me the Spirit in my heart as a guarantee (2 Corinthians 1:22)
663. The God who purchased me to be His own (Ephesians 1:14)
664. The God who ascended to Heaven and descended (John 3:13)
665. The God who closed the winds in His fists (Proverbs 30:4)
666. The God who wrapped the waters in His garment (Proverbs 30:4)
667. The God who established all the ends of the earth (Proverbs 30:4)
668. The God who has called me to share in His eternal glory through Jesus Christ (1 Peter 5:10)
669. The God who calls me to His kingdom and glory (1 Thessalonians 2:12)
670. The God who heals all my diseases (Psalm 103:3; Exodus 15:26)
671. God, the blessed forever (Psalm 21:6)
672. The Lord, worthy of supreme worship and praise (Psalm 96:4; Revelation 4:11)
673. The God of powerful declarations (Psalm 2:7–12)
674. God, the one worthy of all holy dance (Psalms 149:3; 150:4)
675. God, You are Spirit; I worship you in spirit and truth (John 4:23–24)
676. The God who laid the foundations of the earth, and they will never be removed (Psalm 104:5)
677. The God who affirms His upper rooms on the waters (Psalm 104:3)
678. The God who makes the clouds His chariots of war

and who rides on the wings of the wind (Psalm 104:3)

679. The God who redeems me from destruction (Psalm 103:4)
680. The God who affirms me and guards me against evil (Isaiah 41:10)
681. The God who takes revenge (Romans 12:19)
682. The God with the last word (1 Peter 3:22)
683. The God who is coming soon to reward each one according to his work (Revelation 22:12)
684. God, who asks me to be still and know that You are God (Psalm 46:10)
685. The God, from eternity to eternity, You inhabit eternity (Isaiah 43:13)
686. God, the crown of glory (Isaiah 62:3)
687. God, the lovely wreath over my head (Proverbs 4:9)
688. Jesus, the one who is altogether lovely (Song of Solomon 5:15)
689. The God who hides (Isaiah 45:15)
690. The Lord, the high priest over the house of God (Hebrews 10:21)
691. The God of widows (Isaiah 54:4; Psalm 68:5)
692. God, the light that illuminates the gentiles (Isaiah 49:6; Acts 13:47)
693. God, the living rock (1 Peter 2:4)
694. Jesus Christ, the scepter of justice (Hebrews 1:8)
695. God, my perfect mate and spouse (Revelation 21:2–9; Isaiah 54:5; Ephesians 5:25–33)
696. God, the stumbling block for the wicked (Ezekiel 14:3)
697. God (Jesus), the stone of stumbling to unbelievers (1 Peter 2:8)

698. The God who keeps my feet from stumbling (Psalm 66:9)
699. God, the captain of my salvation (Hebrews 2:10)
700. Christ, the desire of all nations (1 John 5:6)
701. God, my eternal God (Psalm 90:1–4; Genesis 21:33)
702. Lord, your word is truth (John 17:17)
703. God, the one who is holy and true (Revelation 3:7)
704. God, the one who has the key of David. What You open, no one can shut; and what You shut, no one can open (Revelation 3:7)
705. God, the glory of Your people (Luke 2:32)
706. God my maker (John 54:5–8; Isaiah 43:15)
707. The God of all families—present, past, and future (Exodus 12:14; Joel 1:3; Ephesians 3:21)
708. The God who vindicates me (Psalm 135:14)
709. The God who commands the winds and they obey You (Luke 8:25)
710. God, the flash of lighting (Ezekiel 1:14)
711. God, the supreme one (Deuteronomy 10:17–22)
712. The God of the seven feasts and celebrations (Zephaniah 3:17; Leviticus 23)
713. The God of perfection (Matthew 5:48)
714. The God of the nations (Psalms 72:11; 86:9)
715. The God of revival (2 Chronicles 7:14; Psalms 119:50; 119:25)
716. The God of the little ones (Matthew 18:10)
717. The God of dominion (Job 25:2)
718. The God of maximum power (Revelation 15:8; Psalm 147:4–5)
719. The God and Creator of the ocean (Proverbs 8:29; Genesis 1:21)

720. The God who holds the key to life and death (Revelation 1:18)
721. The God of the islands (Psalm 97:1)
722. The God who has a count of all my hairs (Luke 12:7)
723. God, my intelligence (Ephesians 3:4)
724. God, who gives me insight (2 Timothy 2:7)
725. God, my revelation (Psalm 27:1)
726. The God of wisdom (James 1:5)
727. God, the one who gives wisdom (Ecclesiastes 2:26)
728. Christ the power and wisdom of God (1 Corinthians 1:24)
729. Jesus, worthy to receive power and wealth and wisdom and might and honor and glory and blessing (Revelation 5:12)
730. Jesus, the Lamb of God who takes away the sin of the world (John 1:29)
731. Jesus, the One who sacrificed His life for me (1 John 3:16; John 3:16)
732. Jesus, the one who bruised the enemy's head (Genesis 3:15)
733. Jesus Christ, the one with the precious and powerful blood (1 Peter 1:19)
734. The God of the Lamb's Book of Life (Revelation 13:8)
735. Jesus, the Lamb that was slain without blemish (Revelation 5:12)
736. Jesus, who is the sinless and spotless Lamb of God (1 Peter 1:19)
737. God, the one sitting on the throne (Revelation 5:13)
738. The God who arms me with strength and power (Psalm 18:32)

739. The Lord who gives strength to His people (Psalm 29:11)
740. God, the strength of the poor needy in distress (Isaiah 25:4)
741. God, the one who renews my strength (Psalm 103:5–7)
742. God, the rock of my strength and my glory (Psalm 62:7)
743. The God who trains my hands for battle and strengthens my arms to draw the bronze bow (Psalm 18:34)
744. God who heals my body and strengthens my bones. (Proverbs 3:8)
745. God, You are almighty in strength (Job 9:4)
746. The God with incredible greatness in power (Ephesians 1:19)
747. The God who speaks into my life (Matthew 4:4)
748. The God who opens my ears to listen (Isaiah 50:4)
749. The God who opens my eyes to see and understand (Psalm 119:18)
750. The God who gives me innovating thoughts (Mark 2:21–22)
751. The God who gives me creativity (Exodus 35:35)
752. The God who fills my mouth with praise (Psalm 71:8)
753. The God of my heart (Psalm 73:26)
754. The God of my health (Psalm 30:2)
755. The God of my hands (Nehemiah 6:9)
756. The God who has rescued me from the depths of death (Psalm 86:13)
757. God, You are, You were, and You will be forever the Lord (Psalms 90:2; 48:14)

758. God, my reason to live (Philippians 1:21; Romans 14:8)
759. The God of wealth and prosperity (Isaiah 66:12; Proverbs 8:18)
760. The God of opportunities (Ephesians 5:16)
761. The great God, His understanding is infinite (Psalm 147:5)
762. God, my inventor (Genesis 5:1)
763. God, my strong fortress (Psalm 18:2)
764. God, Christ in me (Galatians 2:20, 27; John 14:20; Romans 8:10)
765. God, my eternal hope (Titus 3:7)
766. Christ, the hope of glory (Colossians 1:27)
767. The God of hope (Romans 15:13; Romans 8:24)
768. God, my confidence (Philippians 1:6)
769. God, my delight (Psalm 37:4)
770. God, my well-being (John 5:11; Luke 11:28)
771. God, my high place (Habakkuk 3:19)
772. God, my hiding place (Psalm 32:7)
773. God, the unchangeable one (Hebrews 6:17)
774. The God of powerful decrees (Exodus 18:20; 2 Chronicles 34:31)
775. The God who can't be surprised (Ezekiel 11:5; Genesis 3:5)
776. The God who owns all the kingdoms (1 Chronicles 29:11)
777. The God who gives riches (Ecclesiastes 6:2)
778. The God of blessings, the blesser (Numbers 6:24–26)
779. The God of divine purpose (Job 42:2; Romans 8:28; Proverbs 19:21)
780. The God of my destiny (Jeremiah 1:5; Isaiah 55:11)

781. God, You are the air and breath in my lungs (Genesis 2:7; Job 27:3; Ezekiel 37:9; Psalm 150:6)
782. The God of holiness (Leviticus 19:2)
783. Lord, Your instructions are perfect and revive my soul (Psalm 19:7)
784. Lord, Your decrees are trustworthy and make wise the simple (Psalm 19:7)
785. Lord, Your commandments are right and bring joy to my heart (Psalm 19:8)
786. Lord, Your commands are clear and give me insight for a living (Psalm 19:8)
787. The God of mysteries (Deuteronomy 29:29; 1 Timothy 3:16)
788. The God who knows everything (1 John 3:20; Psalm 69:5)
789. The God who knows the past, present, and future (Isaiah 43:18)
790. The God who works in mysterious ways (Isaiah 55:8–9)
791. The Lord who exults over me with loud singing (Zephaniah 3:17)
792. The God who quiets me with His love (Zephaniah 3:17)
793. The God of the day and night (Psalm 42:8)
794. The God who gives me new life in Your love (Zephaniah 3:17)
795. The God who forgives and forgets (Isaiah 43:25)
796. God, a hiding place from the wind (Isaiah 32:2)
797. The Lord who makes me a crown of glory in His hand (1 Peter 5:4)
798. The Lord who makes me a diadem of beauty (Isaiah 61:3)
799. The God who hides Himself (Isaiah 45:15)

800. Lord, Your understanding is infinite (Psalm 147:5)
801. God, the Governor of the universe (Psalm 147:4)
802. God, the Creator of the universe (Genesis 1:1–31
803. Jesus Christ, the sustainer of the universe (Hebrews 1:3)
804. The God with dominion over the universe (Genesis 1:26)
805. The most holy God (Psalm 99:3; 1 Peter 1:16)
806. The just God (2 Thessalonians 1:6)
807. God, the living stone (1 Peter 2:4–8)
808. The great, merciful God (Psalm 145:8)
809. God, the mighty, awesome one (Jeremiah 20:11)
810. God, a rewarder of those who diligently seek You (Hebrews 11:6)
811. God, my shadow from the heat (Isaiah 4:6)
812. God, You are the strong tower that protects me from the enemy (Proverbs 18:10)
813. God, my secure foundation (Isaiah 28:16)
814. God, the ever-present help in trouble (Isaiah 41:4)
815. God, the wall of fire around me (Zechariah 2:5)
816. The God who answers by fire (1 Kings 18:24)
817. The God of the fire (1 Kings 18:24)
818. The God who makes the winds His messengers, and the flames of fire His ministers (Psalm 104:4; Hebrews 1:7)
819. The God with eyes like a flame of fire and feet like polished bronze (Revelation 1:14–15; 2:18; 19:12)
820. The Lord my God, a consuming fire and a jealous God (Deuteronomy 4:24)
821. Lord, Your voice raises flames of fire (Psalm 29)
822. God, the Almighty one (Revelation 11:17)
823. God, the alpha and omega (Revelation 21:6; 22:13)

824. God, the ensign/banner for the nations (Isaiah 5:26)
825. God, the ancient of days (Daniel 7:9)
826. God, the author of peace (1 Corinthians 14:33; John 14:27)
827. God, the blessed and only sovereign (1 Timothy 6:15)
828. God, the Lord of lords (1 Timothy 6:15)
829. Jesus, the bright and morning star (Revelation 22:16)
830. God, the buckler to them that walk uprightly (Proverbs 2:7)
831. The God who is good and upright (Psalm 25:8)
832. The God of relationship (John 1:18; Romans 5:11)
833. Christ, the power of God (1 Corinthians 1:24)
834. God, the confidence of all the ends of the earth (Proverbs 3:26)
835. God, my first love (1 John 4:19)
836. God, the former of all things (Jeremiah 10:16)
837. God, the fountain of living waters; You give to all who are thirsty from Your springs of the water of life (Revelation 21:6)
838. Lord, the fountain of life (Psalm 36:9)
839. The God who holds our breath in His hands (Daniel 5:23)
840. The God who owns all our ways (Daniel 5:23)
841. God, the most high (Hebrews 7:1)
842. God, my maker (Job 36:3)
843. God, the One that was before Abraham, Isaac, and Jacob (Acts 3:13)
844. The God of Abraham, Isaac, and Jacob (Acts 7:32)
845. The God of all comfort (2 Corinthians 1:3)
846. The God of all flesh (Jeremiah 32:27)

847. **Christ, Your glory fills the skies** (Psalm 19:1, Habakkuk 3:3-4, Isaiah 6:3)
848. The God of Hosanna in the Highest (Matthew 21:9)
849. The God of gods (Daniel 2:47)
850. The God of heaven and earth (Psalm 146:6)
851. The God of Jeshurun (upright) (Deuteronomy 33:26–29)
852. God, the fountain of joy and happiness (Isaiah 9:3; Psalm 47:1)
853. God, the Spirit of knowledge (Isaiah 11:2; Daniel 5:12)
854. The God and author of all knowledge (Proverbs 1:7)
855. The God who is perfect in knowledge (Job 36:4)
856. Jesus, the longsuffering one (Ephesians 4:2)
857. Jesus, the one who overcomes the world (1 John 5:5)
858. The Lord who goes out like mighty man of war (Isaiah 42:12)
859. God, the perfect one (Matthew 5:48)
860. God, there is no evil in You (Psalm 92.15)
861. God, everything is okay and perfectly fine in you (Psalm 92:15; Mark 10:27; Philippians 4:13
862. The Lord of my destiny and future (Jeremiah 29:11)
863. The God of my praise (Exodus 15:2; 1 Chronicles 16:25)
864. The God of my salvation (Psalm 62; Isaiah 12:2)
865. The God of consolation (Jeremiah 31:13)
866. The God of the living (Mark 12:27)
867. The God of the spirits of all flesh (Numbers 27:16)

868. The God of the whole earth (Psalm 57:5; Isaiah 40:21–31)
869. The God of my fathers and mothers (Matthew 22:32; Genesis 31:42)
870. God of truth and without iniquity (Deuteronomy 32:4)
871. Lord, the only wise God (Romans 16:27)
872. The God who is ready to forgive (Psalm 86:5)
873. The God who cannot lie (Titus 1:2)
874. The God who comforts those that are cast down (2 Corinthians 7:6)
875. The God who does wonders (Psalm 77:14)
876. The God who formed me (Isaiah 49:5; Psalm 119:73)
877. The God who gives to all men liberally (James 1:5)
878. Jesus of Galilee (Matthew 26:69)
879. Jesus, everything was created through You and for You (Colossians 1:16)
880. Jesus, You existed before all things (Colossians 1:16)
881. Jesus, You hold all creation together (Colossians 1:17)
882. The God who performs all things for me (Psalm 57:2)
883. God, the Lord of all (Romans 10:12)
884. The God who always causes us to triumph in Christ (2 Corinthians 2:14)
885. The God who performs wonders that cannot be fathomed, miracles that cannot be counted. (Job 5:9)
886. The God who fed me all my life until this day (Genesis 2:16; Philippians 4:19; Deuteronomy 8:3)

887. Jesus Christ, who gives us victory over sin and death by His power (1 Corinthians 15:56)
888. The God who gives heed to my prayer (Psalms 61:1; 86:6)
889. The God who answers prayers (John 15:7)
890. Christ the risen one (Matthew 28:5)
891. The God who tests my heart and character (Psalms 105:19; 139:23)
892. God, the guide of my youth (Jeremiah 3:4; Proverbs 2:17)
893. God, the habitation of justice (Jeremiah 50:7)
894. God, who is enthroned from ages past (Psalms 90:2; 93:2)
895. The God who is enthroned on my praises (Psalm 22:3)
896. The God who built all things (Hebrews 3:4)
897. The God of the Ten Commandments (Exodus 20)
898. The God who called me into the grace of Christ (Galatians 1:15)
899. The God who calls for the waters of the sea and pours them out upon the face of the earth (Amos 9:6)
900. Jesus Christ, the first to rise from the dead (Acts 26:23)
901. God, the one who creates the wind (Amos 4:13)
902. The God who creates and forms the mountains (Amos 4:13)
903. The Lord God of the mountains and hills (1 Kings 20:28)
904. The God who melts the mountains beneath his feet (Micah 1:4)
905. The God who declares His thoughts to mankind (Amos 4:13)

906. The God who turns dawn to darkness (Amos 4:13)
907. The God who strides on the heights of the earth (Amos 4:13)
908. Lord God Almighty is your name (Amos 4:13)
909. The God who endured opposition from sinners (Hebrews 12:3)
910. The God who fills all in all (Ephesians 1:23)
911. The God whose names go beyond the alphabet (Philippians 2:9)
912. The God who has given us all we need for a godly life through our knowledge of You (1 Peter 1:3)
913. The God who called us by His own glory and goodness (2 Peter 1:3)
914. The God who has the seven spirits (Revelation 1:4)
915. The God who holds the seven stars in His right hand (Revelation 1:16)
916. The God who can do exceedingly, abundantly above all that we can ask or think (Ephesians 3:20–21)
917. The God who can keep me from falling (Jude 24)
918. The God who can present me faultless before the presence of His glory with exceeding joy (Jude 24)
919. You, the one who is from the beginning (1 John 2:13)
920. Lord, in You all things hold together (Colossians 1:17)
921. The God who is higher than the highest (Ecclesiastes 5:8)
922. The God who is the Holy of Holies (Hebrews 9:3; Exodus 26:34)
923. The God who establishes me with power (2 Corinthians 1:21; Isaiah 40:10)
924. God, the absolute truth (John 14:6; 8:32)

925. The God who keeps me (Psalm 121:5)
926. Jesus Christ, the one who lives forever eternally (John 10:10)
927. The God who makes the seven stars and Orion (Amos 5:8)
928. God, the one who is to be feared (Psalm 89:7)
929. The God who understands all hearts (Proverbs 24:12)
930. The Holy Spirit who raised Jesus from the dead (Romans 8:11)
931. The God who reveals secrets (1 Corinthians 2:10; Deuteronomy 29:29)
932. The God who searches hearts (Romans 8:27)
933. The God who is sitting upon the great majestic throne (Revelation 5:13)
934. The God who speaks from heaven (Hebrews 12:25)
935. The God, with blinding speed and power, that destroys the strong, crushing all their defenses (Amos 5:9)
936. The God who works miracles among us (Galatians 3:5)
937. God, the one who parted the Red Sea (Psalm 136:13)
938. The God who gives life unto the world (John 6:33)
939. The Holy One who anoints me to be part of His royal priesthood (1 Peter 2:9)
940. God, the anchor of my soul (Hebrews 6:19)
941. The God who led His people through the wilderness (Psalm 136:16)
942. The God who searches out the thoughts and intentions of everyone (Revelation 2:23)

943. The God who walks in the midst of the seven golden candlesticks (Revelation 1:12–13)
944. The God who works all things after the counsel of his own will (Ephesians 1:11)
945. God, the health of my countenance (Psalm 43:5)
946. God, Your Spirit that dwells in me (Romans 8:9)
947. God, the horn of my salvation (Psalm 18:2)
948. God, my Jah (Exodus 15:2)
949. The Lord, my hallelujah (Psalm 146:1–10)
950. God, Jehovah (YHWH), the I Am (Exodus 6:2–3; 3:14)
951. The Lord of the Sabbath (Mark 2:28)
952. The Lord God on High (Psalm 92:8)
953. The Lord God Almighty (1 Kings 19:10)
954. The Lord God, the rock of my salvation (2 Samuel 22:47)
955. The Lord God of the holy prophets (Revelation 22:6)
956. The Lord God of truth (John 17:3; Isaiah 65:16)
957. God, the one who gathers (Isaiah 56:8)
958. The Lord of glory (James 2:1)
959. The Lord who owns the entire earth and everything in it (Psalm 24:1)
960. Jesus, the one exalted above all (Psalm 97:9)
961. God, the Lord of the majesty on high (Psalm 93:4)
962. Jesus, the Master (Mark 13:1)
963. God, the mighty God of Jacob (Psalm 132:2)
964. God, You are great goodness (Nehemiah 9:25; Psalm 23:6)
965. God, the most upright (Micah 7:4)
966. God, my hiding place (Psalm 32:7)
967. God, my high tower (Psalm 144:2)
968. Jesus, the salt of the earth (Matthew 5:13)

969. God, my hope in the day of evil (Jeremiah 17:17)
970. God, You are my portion forever (Lamentations 3:24)
971. God, my portion in the land of the living (Psalm 142:5)
972. God, my strong habitation to which I may continually come (Psalm 71:3)
973. God, the rock of ages (1 Corinthians 10:4)
974. God, my potter (Isaiah 64:8)
975. God, the portion of Jacob (Jeremiah 10:16)
976. God, the possessor of heaven and earth (Genesis 14:19)
977. God, the rivers of water in a dry place (Isaiah 32:2)
978. God, my Shiloh, my worship place (Jeremiah 41:5)
979. God, the Spirit of glory (1 Peter 4:14)
980. The Spirit of God, the Holy Ghost (Romans 5:5; Micah 3:8–10)
981. God, the Spirit who flows like a mighty river (Amos 5:24; Isaiah 66:12)
982. Holy Spirit, the baptizer (Acts 2:38–41)
983. God, the Spirit of grace (Zechariah 12:10)
984. Holy Spirit, my helper (John 14:26)
985. Holy Spirit, my intimate friend (James 4:5)
986. Holy Spirit, who fills me with His fruit and spiritual gifts (Galatians 5:22; 1 Corinthians 12; 14; Romans 12:6–10)
987. The Spirit who convicts me of all sin (John 16:8)
988. God, the Spirit of holiness (Romans 1:4)
989. God, the Spirit of life (John 6:63)
990. God, the Spirit of the living God (2 Corinthians 3:3)
991. The Spirit of the Lord (2 Corinthians 3:17)
992. Lord, the living God (Hebrews 10:31)

993. God, the Spirit of truth (John 15:26)
994. God, the sword of excellency and majesty (Deuteronomy 33:29)
995. Jesus, the Amen (Psalm 41:13; Romans 11:36)
996. The eternal Spirit (Hebrews 9:14)
997. God, the glory in the midst of your city (Zechariah 2:5)
998. God, the most high, great, and mighty (Psalm 145:3–7)
999. The Lord, strong and mighty in battle (Psalm 24:8)
1000. The Lord who heals my heart (Psalm 147:3)
1001. The Lord who is in my midst (Deuteronomy 7:21)
1002. The Lord my God, who goes before me (Deuteronomy 31:8)
1003. The Most High over all the earth (Psalm 83:18)
1004. God, the only true God (Jeremiah 10:10; John 17:3)
1005. God, the only wise God (Romans 16:27; Jude 25)
1006. God, the pearl of great price (Matthew 13:46)
1007. God, the incorruptible God (Romans 1:23)
1008. The God enthroned between the cherubim; You alone are God over all kingdoms (2 Kings 19:15)
1009. The God who gives me dignity (Job 40:10; Psalm148:14)
1010. God, my mantle of praise (Isaiah 61:3)
1011. God, my covering (Psalm 32:1–2)
1012. The God of success (Proverbs 16:3)
1013. God, the giver of rest and sweet sleep (Matthew 11:28; Psalm 4:8)
1014. God, the inventor of the highest intelligence
1015. The God who gives me sight to see (Proverbs 29:13)
1016. God, You are my heart and life (Psalm 73:26)

1017. God, You are enough (2 Corinthians 12:9–10)
1018. God, You are my divine health and wellness (Jeremiah 30:17; 1 Corinthians 6:19–20)
1019. God, You train my arms for war (Psalm 144:1–2)
1020. God, You are my designer (Genesis 1:26)
1021. God, You are my reason to live (Romans 14:8)
1022. God, my strong rock (Psalm 31:2)
1023. God, my total confidence (Hebrews 4:16)
1024. God, the one who lives forever eternally (Daniel 12:7; Hebrews 7:24)
1025. God, who loves me and gave Himself for me (Galatians 2:20)
1026. God, who makes the clouds His chariots (Psalm 104:3)
1027. The God who rides on the wings of the wind (Psalm 104:3)
1028. God, the immortal one (1 Timothy 6:16)
1029. God, the one who dwells in unapproachable light (1 Timothy 6:16)
1030. The Lord who possesses honor and eternal dominion (1 Timothy 6:16)
1031. God, the Father who sings over me (Zephaniah 3:17)
1032. God, the one who surrounds me with songs of victory and deliverance (Psalm 32:7)
1033. The God who breathes His Ruach over me and into me (John 20:22)
1034. The Lord, who is in me, and me in him (John 14:20; 17:23)
1035. The God who formed me into His image and likeness (Genesis 1:27)
1036. God, my place of safety (Psalm 91:2)
1037. The God who makes me dwell in safety (Psalm 4:8)

1038. The Lord, who makes me acceptable in His sight (Psalm 19:11–14)
1039. God, the one who rescued me from every trap (Psalm 91:3)
1040. God, the one who protects me from a deadly disease (Psalm 91:3)
1041. God, the one who covers me with His feathers and shelters me with his wings (Psalm 91:4)
1042. God, my shelter in the storm where no evil can conquer me (Psalm 91:9)
1043. God, the one who orders His angels to protect me wherever I go (Psalm 91:11)
1044. The Lord who is robed in majesty and armed with strength (Psalm 93:1)
1045. The God who is greater than we can understand; His years cannot be counted (Job 36:26)
1046. The God who is in love with me (Romans 8:35, 37–39; Psalm 5:11–12)
1047. The God who commanded the morning to appear and caused the dawn to rise in the east (Job 38:12)
1048. The God who counts the number of the stars (Psalm 147:4–5)
1049. The God whose understanding is infinite (Psalm 147:4–5)
1050. The Lord who reigns for eternity (Psalm 146:10)
1051. The God who made the daylight spread to the ends of the earth to bring an end to the night's wickedness (Job 38:12–13)
1052. The God who kept the sea inside its boundaries as it burst from the womb clothed it with clouds and wrapped it in thick darkness (Job 38:8–9)
1053. The God of the pure in heart (Matthew 5:8)
1054. God, the beautiful one (Isaiah 33:17; 28:5)

1055. God, You are my beautiful crown and a glorious diadem (Isaiah 28:5)
1056. The loving God (John 3:16; 1 John 4:19)
1057. God, the one with endless names and attributes (Romans 1:20)
1058. The God who never changes (Numbers 23:19)
1059. The God who never fails me (Hebrews 13:5)
1060. God, Your will is good, pleasing, and perfect (Romans 12:2)
1061. The God who has made everything perfect in its time (Ecclesiastes 3:11)
1062. The Lord, the high and exalted one who lives forever and whose name is holy (Isaiah 57:15)
1063. The God who is with those whose spirits are contrite and humble (Isaiah 57:15)
1064. The God who restores the crushed spirit of the humble and revives the courage of the repentant heart (Isaiah 57:15)
1065. God, the One who gives me laughter (Psalm 126:2)
1066. The God who wipes every tear from my eyes (Revelation 21:4)
1067. The God who is always by my side (Isaiah 41:10)
1068. God, my everything in everything (1 Corinthians 15:28)
1069. God, the solution to everything (Philippians 4:6)
1070. God, the only one that satisfies my soul (Psalms 63; 107:8–9)
1071. The God of all generations (Genesis 17:7; 9:12)
1072. God, the origin of my spirit—You are my origin; I originated in the midst of Your throne (Genesis 2:7)
1073. God, Your kingdom is eternal, unmovable, and indestructible (Daniel 4:4; 34–37)

1074. The God who has no competition and no rival (Philippians 2:9–11; 1 Timothy 1:17)
1075. The God who breaks the pride of princes (Psalm 76:12)
1076. The God who rules with an iron scepter (Revelation 2:27)
1077. God, the one whose throne is forever and ever (Psalm 45:6)
1078. God, Your throne endures forever and ever (Psalm 45:6)
1079. God, You rule with a scepter of justice (Psalm 45:6)
1080. The God who establishes law and order (Exodus 20)
1081. Jesus, the maximum and highest authority (John 17:2; Matthew 28:18)
1082. The God who commands submission to delegated authority (Hebrews 13:17; 1 Peter 2:17–18)
1083. Lord, Your presence is the home of my spirit (Acts 17:28)
1084. Lord, Your word is sweeter than honey (Psalm 119:103)
1085. The God who reveals Yourself to whom You desire (Matthew11:27; Luke 24:32; Ephesians 1:17–18)
1086. Lord, Your presence and words are healing to my soul (Psalm 41:4)
1087. God, Your presence fills me with joy (Acts 2:28)
1088. Lord, Your presence delivers me and gives me freedom (Romans 8:2)
1089. God, the divine architect of all (Psalm 19)
1090. The God who leads me beside peaceful streams (Psalm 23)
1091. God, my peaceful place of security (Isaiah 32:18)

1092. The Lord who prepares a feast for me in the presence of my enemies (Psalm 23:5)
1093. The God who anoints my head with oil until my cup overflows with blessings (Psalm 23:5)
1094. The God who pursues me with His goodness and unfailing love all the days of my life (Psalm 23:6)
1095. The God who keeps His promises of unfailing love (Daniel 9:4)
1096. The God who fulfills His covenant (Daniel 9:4)
1097. The Lord who watches over me and keep me from all harm (Psalm 121)
1098. The God who gives me a dance (Psalms 30:11)
1099. God, my threshing floor (Micah 4:12; Matthew 3:12)
1100. Holy Spirit, my empowerment (Acts 1:8)
1101. The Holy Spirit, my fiercely jealous lover (James 4:5)
1102. God, the reason for my Yadah, I praise you reverently (2 Samuel 22:50)
1103. God, you are my Towdah, I give thanks to you, my Lord (Leviticus 7:12)
1104. God, my Halal, my highest praise and hallelujah (Psalm 146:1; 2 Chronicles 20:19)
1105. God, my Barak, I kneel before you with reverence (Ephesians 3:14; Judges 5:2)
1106. God, my Tehillah, my spontaneous new song (2 Chronicles 20:22; Psalm 33:3; Ephesians 5:19–20)
1107. God, my Shabach, the loud praise of my heart (Psalms 63:3; 117:1)
1108. God, my Zamar, the singing and praise of my soul (Psalms 21:13; 144:9)
1109. God, your name is a strong tower (Proverbs 18:10)
1110. The God of reverence and respect (1 Peter 1:15)

1111. The God of the sacred altar (Matthew 23:19)
1112. The God of the sacred and holy (Psalms 96:9; Isaiah 6:3)
1113. The God of humility (Luke 22:26; Matthew 20:28)
1114. The God worthy of eternal worship (Revelation 5:1–14; 19:1–8)
1115. The God of dreams and visions (Daniel 1:17; Numbers 12:6)
1116. The Lord God of Hosts (Amos 4:13; Isaiah 5:16; Jeremiah 31:23)
1117. God, holy, holy, holy are You, Lord God, the Almighty (Revelation 4:8)
1118. Lord, Your name is lovely and worthy to be celebrated with music (Psalm 135:3)
1119. The God of loyalty (Deuteronomy 7:12)
1120. The God with the crown of glory (Isaiah 62:3)
1121. The God of unity (John 17:11)
1122. God, You are my prophetic mantle (2 Kings 2:13–14)
1123. Lord, You are my mantle of righteousness (Isaiah 61:10)
1124. Lord, You are my garment of salvation (Isaiah 61:10)
1125. God, the blesser of all time and ages (Deuteronomy 28; Numbers 6:24–25)
1126. The God of grace and peace (Nehemiah 9:31; Judges 6:24)
1127. The Father who knows all my needs always (Matthew 6:32)
1128. God, the Spirit who guides and instructs me into all truth (John 16:13)
1129. The God who owns the mountain peaks (Psalm 95:4)

1130. The God whose steadfast love is eternal for those who fear you (Psalm 103:17)
1131. The God who opens His hand to satisfy the desire of every living thing (Psalm 145:16)
1132. The God who instructs me (Psalm 16:7)
1133. The God who directs my steps and delights in every detail of my life (Psalm 37:23)
1134. The Lord who will not abandon Your people, because that would dishonor Your great name (1 Samuel 12:22)
1135. The magnificent God who can never be praised enough (Psalm 145:3–12; Deuteronomy 4:34; Psalm 48:2)
1136. The God with no boundaries to His greatness (Psalm 145:3–12)
1137. God, you are gentleness (Psalm 18:35)
1138. God, the intimate one (James 4:8)
1139. God, the author of the Bible (2 Timothy 3:16)
1140. The God of the cherubim and archangels (Jude 9; Genesis 3:24)
1141. The God and designer of the ark of the covenant (Exodus 25:10–22)
1142. God, the architect of Noah's Ark (Genesis 7)
1143. The God of the Scriptures (2 Timothy 3:16–17)
1144. The God of Selah (Psalms 3:2–4; 24:6)
1145. God Most High, the God who accomplishes all things for me (Psalms 57:2; 7:10)
1146. The God who waters the earth and prepares it for a bountiful harvest of grain (Psalm 65:9)
1147. The God who crowns the year with goodness (Psalm 65:11)
1148. The One who overflows with richness wherever He is (Psalm 65:11)

1149. The God who has done awe-inspiring deeds for Adam's descendants (Psalm 66:5)
1150. The God who tests us and refines us as silver is refined. (Psalm 66:10)
1151. Lord, You are the joy of my salvation (Psalm 51:12)
1152. The God who is pleased with sacrifices offered in the right spirit (Psalm 51:19)
1153. The God who gives me the desires of my heart when I delight in You (Psalm 37:4)
1154. The Lord who just laughs at the wicked, for He sees their day of judgment coming (Psalm 37:13)
1155. The Lord who takes care of the godly and innocent (Psalm 37:17–18)
1156. The Lord who will give me an inheritance that will last forever (Psalm 37:18)
1157. The God who blesses the godly to possess the land (Psalm 37:29)
1158. God, the One who directs the steps of the godly (Psalm 37:23)
1159. The Lord who delights in every detail of my life (Psalm 37:23)
1160. The God who holds me by His hand so if I stumble, I will never fall (Psalm 37:22–24)
1161. The God who honors me when I put my hope in You (Psalm 37:34)
1162. The Lord who prepares a wonderful future for those who love peace (Psalm 37:37)
1163. The Father who never leaves or abandons me from day one (Deuteronomy 31:6)
1164. The God who never gives up on me (Psalm 136)
1165. Jesus, the one who made us a kingdom of priests for God his Father (Revelation 1:6)

1166. God, Your voice is like a trumpet blast (Revelation 1:10)
1167. God, the one who holds the seven stars in Your right hand (Revelation 2.1)
1168. God, the one who gives me authority over all the nations (Revelation 2.26)
1169. God the one who gives me the authority to overcome all the power of the enemy (Luke 10:19)
1170. God, the limitless and endless one (Matthew 19:26)
1171. Lord, You are the one who heals me and lifts my head with honor (1 Samuel 2:30; Psalm 3:3; John 12:26)
1172. You are the Chief Shepherd (1 Peter 5:4)
1173. Lord, the one who deserves reverence and respect (Leviticus 26:2; Psalm 119:15)
1174. The Lord who practices steadfast love, justice, and righteousness in the earth (Jeremiah 9:24)
1175. The God of the immense ocean (Psalm 93:4)
1176. The God of the storms and whirlwinds (Job 38:1)
1177. The God whose workmanship is marvelous (Psalm 139:14)
1178. The Lord who has precious thoughts about me (Psalm 139:17–18)
1179. The One who fearfully and wonderfully made me (Psalm 139:14)
1180. God, the one who is still with me when I wake up every morning (Psalm 139:18
1181. God, the one who is all-sufficient (Colossians 1:13–20)
1182. Lord, the God of the New Covenant (Jeremiah 31:31–34; Isaiah 42:6)

1183. The God and Creator of the angels (Colossians 1:16; Genesis 2:1)
1184. Jesus, the one who will come with the clouds of heaven (Revelation 1:7; Daniel 7:13)
1185. Lord, You are worthy to receive glory, honor, and power (Revelation 4:11)
1186. The God who exalts Himself as head over all (1 Chronicles 29:11)
1187. The Lord who owns greatness (1 Chronicles 29:11)
1188. The Lord who owns the power (1 Chronicles 29:11 Psalm 62:11)
1189. The Lord who owns the glory (1 Chronicles 29:11)
1190. The Lord who owns the victory (1 Chronicles 29:11)
1191. The Lord who owns the majesty (1 Chronicles 29:11)
1192. The Lord who owns the riches (1 Chronicles 29:12)
1193. The Lord, the source of honor and wealth (1 Chronicles 29:12)
1194. The God who rules over all things (1 Chronicles 29:12)
1195. Lord, in Your hands are power and mighty strength (1 Chronicles 29:12)
1196. The Lord with a glorious name (1 Chronicles 29:13)
1197. The Lord, glorious in holiness, awesome in splendor (Exodus 15:11)
1198. The God of the holy city, the new Jerusalem (Revelation 21:2)
1199. The God who makes all things new (Revelation 21:5; 2 Corinthians 5:17–18)

1200. The God and Creator of the twelve pearly gates (Revelation 21:21)
1201. The God and Creator of every kind of precious stone (Revelation 21:19)
1202. Jesus Christ, the one who is coming soon (Revelation 3:11)
1203. The Lord with the seven Spirits of God (Revelation 5:6)
1204. The Lord who is invincible in battle (Psalm 24:8)
1205. The One who is the Amen. (Revelation 3:14)
1206. Jesus, the victorious, who sat with the Father on His throne (Revelation 3:21; Hebrews 8:1)
1207. God, the one sitting on the throne, was as brilliant as gemstones like jasper and carnelian (Revelation 4:3)
1208. Lord, Your throne is circled with the glow of an emerald-like rainbow (Revelation 4:3)
1209. The God who controls the course of world events (Daniel 2:21)
1210. The God who gives wisdom to the wise (Daniel 2:21)
1211. The God who gives knowledge to the scholars (Daniel 2:21)
1212. The God who gives me wisdom and strength (Daniel 2:23)
1213. The God who puts Your laws in my mind and writes them on my heart (Hebrews 8:10)
1214. Lord, you are the One who builds Your Church (Matthew 16:18)
1215. The One who made the heavenly lights (Psalm 136:7)
1216. Lord, Your Name is lovely and fragrant! (Song 1:3)

1217. Lord, You are the most beautiful Name (Psalm 27:4)
1218. Lord, my God, You are an amazing God (Psalm 68:35)
1219. God, whose names are beyond the letters of the alphabet (John 21:25)
1220. God, the master, chief musician of all times (Psalm 150:1-6; 1 Chronicles 16:42;1 Chronicles 25:1)
1221. God, the Creator of music (Psalm 32:7; Isaiah 6:1–7)
1222. The God of the psalmists and Levites (2 Chronicles 5:12; Numbers 8:14-16; 1 Chronicles 23:24-25)
1223. God, the best singer forever (Zephaniah 3:17)
1224. God, You are my adoration (Psalm 95:6: Psalm 29:2)
1225. Lord, You are the God of the Church (Matthew 16:18; 1 Corinthians 1:2; Ephesians 5:25)
1226. God, the greatest and best artist of all time (Genesis 1–2:4; Job 40:15–41:34)
1227. The God of holy legacy (Psalm 111:9)
1228. The great Engineer of the world (Genesis 1-5)
1229. God, the Creator of colors and fragrances (Genesis 9.13–16; Revelation 4.3; 10:1)
1230. The God of the rain and snow (Job 37:6; Leviticus 26:4; Psalm 147:16)
1231. 12.The God of the spring and summer (Genesis 8:22; Deuteronomy 11:34; Psalm 104:10; Zechariah 10:1)
1232. The God of the fall and winter (Job 37:5–6)
1233. The God of the stars (1 Corinthians 15:41; Isaiah 40:26; Matthew 2:2)

1234. The God of Mars and Jupiter (Acts 14:8–18; 17:22–23)
1235. The God of the sun and the moon (Genesis 1:14–16; Psalm 74:16)
1236. The God and Creator of the creeks, rivers, and lakes (Genesis 1:6–10; 2:10–14; Psalm 65:9; Revelation 22:1)
1237. The God of the water I drink (Genesis 1:2; Isaiah 49:10)
1238. The God of the islands (Genesis 1:9-10; 2 Peter 3:5; Ezekiel 26:18; Psalm 97:1)
1239. The God of the flowers (Song of Solomon 2:12; Luke 12:27)
1240. The God of the cascades (Isaiah 41:18; 61:11; Psalm 42:7)
1241. The Lord who weeps and laughs with me, my friend (Genesis 21:6; Luke 6:21; Psalm 126:2–3; Jeremiah 33:11; Isaiah 53:3–4)
1242. The God who always makes a way (Isaiah 43:16,19; Proverbs 3:5-6)
1243. The God who makes the sun and the moon shine (Jeremiah 31:35; Genesis 1:16–18; Psalm 8:3; 136:7–9; 148:3)
1244. The God of the rocks (Exodus 24:4; Deuteronomy 8:7–9; Psalm 31:3)
1245. The God of the gardens and trees (Psalm 1:3; Genesis 2:9; Psalm 104:16)
1246. The God of the beautiful butterflies (Genesis 1:20; Psalm 104:24-25; Matthew 6:26)
1247. The God of my pets (Psalm 50:10–11; 104:10-14; 145:9; Jonah 4:11)
1248. The God of the hills (Ezekiel 6:3; Proverbs 8:25; Psalm 50:10–12)

1249. The God and Creator of the mountains and valleys (1 Kings 20:28; Psalm 36:6)
1250. The God of the beach and the sand (Genesis 22:17)
1251. The God of the wind (Psalm 107:25; Luke 8:25)
1252. The God of energy and vitality (Ephesians 3:16; Judges 16; 1 Samuel 30:6)
1253. The God of the mountain mines (Deuteronomy 8:7–9; Jeremiah 17:3)
1254. The One who made this day (Psalm118:24)
1255. The God of beauty (Psalm 27:4)
1256. The God of relaxation (Mark 6:31; Psalm 46:10; Matthew 8:24; Psalm 3:5; 23:1–6; 127:2)
1257. The God of the animals (Genesis 1:20–25)
1258. The Creator of the fruits and vegetables (Genesis 1:11; Leviticus 26:4)
1259. God, the strength of the strong (Psalm 46:1: 81:1; Judges 16)
1260. God, the inventor of my personality (Genesis 1:26–28; 2 Peter 1:3–4)
1261. God, You gave me fingers to play music for You (Genesis 4:21)
1262. God, my fountain of rejuvenation (Psalm 103:5; Psalm 91:16; Romans 8:11; Isaiah 40:31)
1263. The God of cheer (Psalm 21:6)
1264. God, my vitality (Ephesians 3:16; Judges 16; 1 Samuel 30:6)
1265. God, my business partner, and my teammate (Romans 8:14; Galatians 5:17–18)
1266. God, the champion of all time (Isaiah 19:20–21; Jeremiah 20:11; Colossians 2:14–15)
1267. God, my delight (Psalm 37:4)
1268. The God who counts all my hairs (Luke 12:7)

1269. God, the author of all authors (Hebrews 12:2)
1270. The God of numbers and symbols (Numbers 10:10)
1271. Jesus, Your name is power and hope (Acts 3:6)
1272. The God who knew me before I was formed in my mother's womb (Jeremiah 1:5)
1273. Lord, You are the One who edifies me (Psalm 127:1; 1 Corinthians 14:4)
1274. You are my Beloved One (Song of Solomon 6:1–3)
1275. God, there is only one of You (Mark 12:29; Deuteronomy 6:4)
1276. God, the most Famous One (Philippians 2:9; 1 Kings 8:
1277. God, the most Eloquent One (Romans 11:33; Job 12:13; Colossians 2:2-3)
1278. God, You are the definition of beauty (Psalm 27:4; Psalm 50:2; 90:17; Ecclesiastes 3:11; Isaiah 33:17;Ezekiel 27:3)
1279. God, You are cool (Psalm 104:1; 145:3; Exodus 3:1-6; 1 Kings 17:7-24; Mark 1:40-42; John 11:1-44)
1280. You are the Creator and designer of all DNA (Genesis 2:7, 21–24)
1281. You are the God of health (Jeremiah 30:17; Exodus 15:26; Psalm 103:2-3; James 5:14-15)
1282. You are the definition of goodness (Psalm 34:8; 100:5; Exodus 34:6; Psalm 145:9; 1 Chronicles 16:34)
1283. You are the definition and embodiment of beautiful perfection (Psalm 50:2; Psalm 27:4)
1284. You are the definition of perfect beauty (Psalm 27:4; 50:2; 90:17; Ecclesiastes 3:11; Isaiah 33:17; Ezekiel 27:3)

1285. You are the very definition of love and kindness (John 3:16;1 John 4:8)
1286. You are the very definition of the fruit of the Spirit (Galatians 5:22–23)
1287. You are the very definition of perfect peace (John 14:27)
1288. You are the definition of perfect, loving justice (Psalm 10:14–18; 2 Samuel 22:31; Matthew 5:47)
1289. You are way more than we know of You (Isaiah 55:8-9; Job 11:7-9; 1 Corinthians 2:9; Psalm 139:6)
1290. God, You are ____________________________ (write something here God has shown you in your walk with Him)

IN CONCLUSION

Knowing Him should be a lifelong commitment. On this journey, it's crucial to keep learning more about His names, titles, and character traits throughout our lives. As we persist in seeking Him, we will indeed find Him. This is His will and desire.

Walking in the intimate knowledge of God stands at the core of revival worship in these last days.

You cannot genuinely and significantly worship a God you don't know or lack the desire to know. To worship Him in spirit and truth, it is imperative to give yourself entirely to Him and continually deepen your understanding of who He is each day, like a bride preparing to meet her Bridegroom, Christ. It is a continuous courtship between the bride and our divine Bridegroom.

Only this intentional worship—in spirit and truth—has

the power to ignite true revival. Such worship alone will usher us into His mighty glory and fire in these last days!

"But the time is coming—indeed it's here now—when true worshipers will worship the Father in spirit and in truth. The Father is looking for those who will worship him that way. For God is Spirit, so those who worship him must worship in spirit and in truth.""

(John 4:23–24, NLT)

Testimonials

Pastor Earl R, MN

Reviewed in the United States on January 10, 2022

Revival Worshipers for the Last Days brings such a timely and practical message, as God prepares us for great end-time Harvest. Yolandita's message rings true through her transparency about her own personal struggles and challenges as God has shaped within her a worshipper's heart. Her vision to raise up revival worshipers is so needed. Yolandita's book inspires me to be one of them.

Pastora Luz A, MN

Reviewed in the United States on May 26, 2022

A book that takes you to the heart of God. This book is an excellent resource for a worshipper. I recommend it.

Pastor Juan V, TX

Reviewed in the United States on October 23, 2021

Captivating! This book has been a blessing! the transparency of someone having a revelation from God and sharing it with us, is priceless. this book is also challenging because right when we think that we have learned enough, it challenges us to step out of our complacency! I am reminded that God is still at work, He is still speaking, God is looking for someone that would want to be taken on a journey! so let's go. Great book!

Jeanne R, MN

Reviewed in the United States on September 25, 2021

I am thankful I read this book! Revival Worshipers for the Last Days" is an important book for our time. With so many distractions, it reminds us who we are and the reason for our existence. Yolandita Colon's testimony, teaching and personal observations bring attention to the key element of what the world needs the most of today. Her writing is poignant and personal, covered in truth and the light that comes from truth. We can all read and learn while being encouraged and equipped. I am thankful for this book!

Anonymous Amazon Customer

Reviewed in the United States on January 2, 2023

Filled with revelations, wisdom, and deep knowledge of God. Immediately, just within the first few pages, I was hooked because I felt the same hunger as the author described. This book encouraged me to dive deeper into God and press into Him even when there are trials, blocks, or unknown circumstances in the future. I haven't even finished it yet, but the Lord has used this book and its revelations to encounter me powerfully multiple times already. If you want to go deeper with the Lord and encounter Him in new ways, get this book. Recommend!

Acknowledgments

In revising this edition, I am profoundly thankful for the unwavering loving support of my husband, Herman, and the invaluable contributions from David Sluka, Pastor Nathanael White, William Rulli, and Yvonne Parks. Their efforts were foundational to both the original and this updated version. While the support landscape has evolved since the first edition, the impact of all who've contributed to this journey remains deeply appreciated.

You can contact Yolandita at www.YolanditaColon.com.

About the Author

Yolandita Colón emerges as a distinguished organic visionary in the realm of prophetic revival worship, known for her profound communion with God and her gift for transforming this connection into life-changing experiences for others. Her spiritual journey, filled with powerful encounters with God from an early age and a transformative vision she received from Jesus in 2009, stands as a vibrant testament to the essence of true worship.

As an ordained minister and the innovative founder of the itinerant worship seminars schools *Selah*, she has spent over two decades empowering a new generation of worship leaders with the wisdom gleaned from her journey with God. She is the author of several books, including "El Asesino del Avivamiento" (The Killer of Revival), a deep analysis of the obstacles to spiritual awakening, and "The Almighty I Am," which is her latest publication following the book you hold in your hands.

Her ministry transcends through "The Father's Songs," a live prophetic worship album flooded with heavenly melodies, inviting listeners to a deeper communion with the Heavenly Father. With a Bachelor of Science degree in Music from North Central University, Minneapolis, complemented by extensive music training from Southwest Missouri State

University, Yolandita's wisdom and experience enrich her spiritual leadership.

Together with her husband, Dr. Herman Colón, she has led two congregations for more than twenty-two years of full-time ministry, marking a lifetime commitment to nurturing faith, community, and the transformative power of worship in spirit and truth. Residing in Minnesota, Yolandita continues to be a beacon of inspiration and a catalyst for spiritual renewal through her teachings, her worship, and her unwavering faith.

Visit her Website: YolanditaColon.com

- facebook.com/YOLANDITAORGANICWORSHIP
- instagram.com/Yolandita_colon
- tiktok.com/@AlmightyIAM
- youtube.com/yolanditacolon7095

Endnotes

4. His Presence is Our Origin

1. Augustine's confessions

5. Created to Bring God Glory

1. *Dr. Trimm, Facebook post, https://www.facebook.com/drtrimm/posts/1914029228610064. From the series, "The DNA of Destiny."*

7. Revival Worshipers Filled with the Holy Spirit

1. Merriam-Webster

23. Struck Down, but Not Destroyed

1. *https://app.worshipu.com/library/why-so-wild*
2. *dictionary.com*

24. The Tones of The Throne Will Cost You

1. I AM: 365 Names and Attributes of God, John Paul Jackson

The Glorious Nature of Our God

1. Yahweh is our God - I Am Who I Am - Tim Mackie (The Bible Project), Tim Mackie Archives channel, https://youtu.be/QcY9fCtTv-4

www.ingramcontent.com/pod-product-compliance
Lightning Source LLC
LaVergne TN
LVHW010651110826
845149LV00014B/3025